Job's Journey

CRITICAL STUDIES IN THE HEBREW BIBLE

Edited by

Anselm C. Hagedorn   Nathan MacDonald   Stuart Weeks

Humboldt Universität   *University of Cambridge*   *Durham University*
zu Berlin

Job's Journey

Stations of Suffering

Manfred Oeming
and
Konrad Schmid

Winona Lake, Indiana
Eisenbrauns
2015

Library of Congress Cataloging-in-Publication Data

Oeming, Manfred, author.
Job's journey : stations of suffering / Manfred Oeming and Konrad
   Schmid.
      pages   cm. — (Critical studies in the Hebrew Bible ; number 2)
   Includes bibliographical references and indexes.
   ISBN 978-1-57506-399-7 (pbk. : alk. paper)
   1. Bible. Job—Criticism, interpretation, etc.   I. Schmid, Konrad,
1965– author.   II. Title.
   BS1415.52.O455   2015
   223'.106—dc23
                                                          2015035856

The paper used in this publication meets the minimum requirements of the American
National Standard for Information Sciences—Permanence of Paper for Printed Library
Materials, ANSI Z39.48–1984. ⊚™

Contents

Foreword

The Book of Job is an important contribution to the canon of world literature. It narrates the thoughts, conflicts, and development of an individual who is suffering from intense pain and misery. Using vivid imagery and language, it pursues theological reflection with an almost scary honesty while illuminating the various stages any suffering individual and those around him will go through. It analyzes paradigmatic problems of being human. It is no surprise that great thinkers (such as Kant, Kierkegaard, Jaspers, and Ricoeur) have turned to this book again and again,[1] while suggesting very different interpretations of its content. Within Old Testament scholarship, the book has caused many controversies and given rise to conflicting hypotheses.[2] In order to understand the diversity of the discourses in contemporary scholarship and in order to realize the position taken in the present essay we provide this short introduction.

1. In spite of many divergent proposals, the *structure* of the book is not very complicated. A clear chiasm seems to underlie the structure, which quite likely indicates a thoroughgoing unity that can easily be shown.

---

1. See W. Strolz "Die Hiobinterpretation bei Kant, Kierkegaard und Bloch," *Kairos* 23 (1981) 75–87; M. Oeming, "Paul Ricoeur als Ausleger des Alten Testaments—unter besonderer Berücksichtigung seiner Interpretation des Buches Hiob," *EvT* 73 (2013) 245–57.

2. For an overview, see H.-P. Müller, *Das Hiobproblem: Seine Stellung und Entstehung im Alten Orient und Alten Testament* (EdF 84; Darmstadt: Wissenschaftliche Buchgesellschaft, 1978; 3rd ed., 1995); C. Newsom, "Re-considering Job," *CBR* 5 (2007) 155–82; J. van Oorschot, "Die Entstehung des Hiobbuches," in *Das Buch Hiob und seine Interpretationen: Beiträge zum Hiob-Symposium auf dem Monte Verità vom 14.–19. August 2005* (ed. T. Krüger et al.; ATANT 88; Zurich: TVZ, 2007) 165–84; L. Schwienhorst-Schönberger, "Das Buch Ijob," in: E. Zenger and C. Frevel (eds.), *Einleitung in das Alte Testament* (Studienbücher Theologie; 8th ed.; Stuttgart, 2012), 414–27; A. Pelham (*Contested Creations in the Book of Job: The-World-as-It-Ought-and-Ought-Not-to-Be* [BibInt 113; Leiden: Brill, 2012] 21) argues that the book lends itself to many divergent interpretations and, therefore, "we may not be able to say what the text means in any kind of nonarbitrary way."

1–2 Prologue: Job's fortune—heavenly assembly—Job's misfortune (prose)

  3 Job curses the day of his birth (poetry)

      4–27: three dialogues (poetry)
      Debates between Job and his friends:
      Job vs. Eliphaz of Teman,
      Job vs. Bildad of Schuach
      Job vs. Zophar of Naamah;

          28 Song of wisdom

      29–41: three monologues (poetry)
      29–31: Job's defense and accusation against God
      32–37: Elihu's defense of God
      38–41: God's speech

  42:1–6 Job's retraction of his curse (poetry)

42:7–17: Epilogue: Restoration of Job's fortune (prose)

---

2. Despite this seemingly clear structure, *many difficult questions remain*. These are the ten most important:

1. How do we explain the move from prose to poetry and back? Does this difference suggest multiple authors?
2. The prose framework depicts Job as someone who humbly accepts his fate. The poetic texts, however, portray Job as a rebel who criticizes God almost to the point of blasphemy. Does this suggest multiple authors?
3. The prose text describes Job as a nomad like Abraham, Isaac, and Jacob. The poetic texts show him to a wealthy urbanite.
4. How are we to understand that the *satan*, who appears as the central antagonist in chapters one and two is never mentioned again?
5. The debates between Job and his friends repeat the same arguments over and over again. Toward the end, the debate dissolves completely. Is the text corrupt?
6. With Elihu, the text introduces a completely new character who had previously not been mentioned. Neither Job nor his friends reacts in any way to this young man's lengthy speech (chapters 32–37). Is it a secondary addition to the text?
7. God's answers do not fit Job's questions. Are they even intended as answers or are they theological commentaries by a later redactor?

8. God's answers develop over several stages. In the middle of one speech, God initiates a second speech. Are these oddities indications of later expansions?

9. Throughout the book, Job is criticized for his presumptuous attacks against God. In the end, however, God praises him and justifies all that he has said. Can this tension be the result of the same author?

10. How are we to understand the mixture of different speakers, moods, and genres? Is the book even trying to give *one* answer to the problem of theodicy?

3. *How can we solve these problems?* The consensus of German scholarship argues that these issues demand a source-critical approach to the book. We face the task of reconstructing an "original Job"—a text that was expanded and added to over the centuries. The models suggested to understand this growth process are becoming ever more complex. A prominent voice comes from Otto Kaiser,[3] with his students and followers, who propose up to seven different stages of textual growth.[4] Scholarship in English-speaking contexts tend to assume more of a literary unity. The most recent commentary by C. Leong Seow proposes that even the Elihu speeches are not a secondary addition to the text;[5] he assumes the literary unit of the whole book. Childs also assumes complete literary unity.[6] The authors of this book also move in this direction. It seems to us that composition of the book is deliberately aimed at engaging the readers in a sometimes confusing and unsettling discourse in order to provoke them to reexamine their own insights into self and God.

---

3. O. Kaiser, *Das Buch Hiob: übersetzt und eingeleitet* (Stuttgart: Radius, 2006).

4. Such as J. van Oorschot, *Gott als Grenze: Eine literar- und redaktionsgeschichtliche Studie zu den Gottesreden des Hiob-Buches* (BZAW 170; Berlin: de Gruyter, 1987); idem, "Die Entstehung des Hiobbuches," in T. Krüger et al. (eds.), *Das Buch Hiob und seine Interpretation: Beiträge zum Hiob-Symposium auf dem Monte Verità vom 14.–19. August 2005* (AThANT 88; Zurich, 2007), 165–84; M. Witte, *Vom Leiden zur Lehre: Der dritte Redegang (Hiob 21–27) und die Redaktionsgeschichte des Hiobbuches* (BZAW 230; Berlin: de Gruyter, 1994); W.-D. Syring, *Hiob und sein Anwalt: Die Prosatexte des Hiobbuches und ihre Rolle in seiner Redaktions- und Rezeptionsgeschichte* (BZAW 336; Berlin: de Gruyter, 2004); U. Nõmmik, *Die Freundesreden des ursprünglichen Hiobdialogs: Eine form- und traditionsgeschichtliche Studie* (BZAW 410; Berlin: de Gruyter, 2010); D. Opel, *Hiobs Anspruch und Widerspruch: Die Herausforderungsreden Hiobs (Hi 29–31) im Kontext frühjüdischer Ethik* (WMANT 127; Neukirchen-Vluyn: Neukirchener, 2010); R. M. Wanke, *Praesentia Dei: Die Vorstellungen von der Gegenwart Gottes im Hiobbuch* (BZAW 421; Berlin: de Gruyter, 2013).

5. C. L. Seow, *Job 1–21: Interpretation and Commentary* (Illuminations; Grand Rapids: Eerdmans, 2013).

6. B. S. Childs, *Introduction to the Old Testament as Scripture* (Philadelphia: Augsburg Fortress, 2010); J. P. Fokkelman, *The Book of Job in Form: A Literary Translation with Commentary* (SSN 58; Leiden, 2012).

Even if we are not able to pursue the following line of thought in detail in this volume, it also seems to us that the complex structure of the Book of Job might also be understood as a counseling process. A psychologically well-experienced author leads his readers through paradigmatic reactions to suffering and death.

4. *When was the book written?* The terminus a quo cannot be earlier than the exile (especially when assuming that Job stands collectively for Israel as a whole, when noticing Assyrian influences, or considering the allusion in Ezek 14:14, 20).[7] A postexilic date is even more plausible, especially because the *satan* is a late Old Testament development. Neither should a full-blown reflection on theodicy be expected any earlier. Because of philosophical influences and many scriptural allusions,[8] we might even assume the Hellenistic era as the best historical location for the book. The latest possible date is marked by Jesus Sirach (180 BCE) because it refers to the book of Job (Sir 49:9). Many propose a separation between an older folktale (1:1–3; 2; 42:7–17) and a later poetic text; this is rather unlikely. The Septuagint (Greek) version of the book, which has appropriately taken on considerable importance in recent scholarship on the book of Job, has significant omissions of ca. 350 lines and (probably) consists of a conscious abbreviation of the difficult Hebrew *Vorlage*. However, the Septuagint also contains two larger expansions in 2:10 and 42:17 that should be investigated in detail.[9]

5. *To which genre does the book belong?* An important context for understanding the book is its function within the community for which it was written. There is no consensus on this question. Some see Job as the greatest of all psalms of lament.[10] Others assume a stylized court drama[11] or a wisdom tract.[12] Currently, the idea that Job is a theatrical play is gaining followers.[13] There is disagreement over whether it is a comedy with a

---

7. R. Heckl, *Vom Gottesfürchtigen zum Repräsentanten Israels: Studien zur Buchwerdung des Hiobbuches und zu seinen Quellen* (FAT 70; Tübingen: Mohr Siebeck, 2012).

8. See K. Dell and W. Kynes, *Reading Job Intertextually* (LHB/OTS 574; London: Continuum, 2012).

9. M. Witte "Job: Das Buch Ijob / Hiob," in *Septuaginta Deutsch: Erläuterungen und Kommentare zum griechischen Alten Testament* (ed. M. Karrer and W. Kraus; Stuttgart: Deutsche Bibelgesellschaft, 2011) 2:2041–126.

10. C. Westermann, *Der Aufbau des Buches Hiob: Mit einer Einführung in die neuere Hiobforschung von Jürgen Kegler* (Calwer Theologische Monographien 6; Stuttgart: Calwer, 1977).

11. H. Richter, *Studien zu Hiob: Der Aufbau des Hiobbuches dargestellt an den Gattungen des Rechtslebens* (Theologische Arbeiten 11; Berlin: EVA, 1959).

12. Müller, *Das Hiobproblem.*

13. B. Klinger, *Im und durch das Leiden lernen: Das Buch Ijob als Drama* (BBB 155; Hamburg: Philo, 2007).

highly ironic portrayal of all cast members or a tragedy aimed at portray-
ing the unsolvable predicaments of human fate.[14] Perhaps the material
was never performed but was intended as "reading drama"[15] for private
use and debate. Taking a more practical approach, other scholars see the
book as some form of self-help book—whether this be a guide for the per-
plexed, a medical compendium on dealing with the psychological effects
of illness,[16] or a counseling manual for traumatized individuals in their
physical and psychological misery.[17]

6. *Are there contemporary parallels in Israel's surroundings?* It remains
a paradigm of contemporary historical-critical interpretation to read a text
in the context of its ancient Near East parallels.[18] We find many parallels to
the book of Job in Egyptian, Mesopotamian, and Greek literature.

7. *Where was the book written?* Clear indications for the place of au-
thorship as well as the place of "application" are absent. Intellectual crises
in Jerusalem are often presumed among those who were in close contact
with the Temple but were distant from it in their point of view; otherwise
how could the book have been received into the canon? A serious candi-
date is also Teman, because this city in the Arabian desert also contained
one of Nabonidus' libraries, which would have provided the necessary
intellectual assets. Its milieu, with a mixture of city-dwellers and nomads,
is easily comprehensible. In any case, it remains surprising that the book of
Job was accepted into the canon of holy writings. For one, its hero is not
an Israelite but, instead, a foreigner from Uz. Second, its theology is very
demanding and often provocative. Third, no simple solution is propagated
but difficult thought processes are required of the reader. These factors do
not usually lead to extensive popularity.

8. *What basic theological issues does the book address?* The book of Job
touches on several fundamental theological issues. The question of *theodicy* is of primary concern: How can God allow so much evil in the world?
Is not the suffering of any righteous individual a scandal, a great blemish

---

14. K. Dell, *The Book of Job as Sceptical Literature* (BZAW 197; Berlin: de Gruyter, 1991).
15. M. Köhlmoos, *Das Auge Gottes: Textstrategie im Hiobbuch* (FAT 25; Tübingen: Mohr Siebeck, 1999).
16. A. M. Gotto, "Suffering, Medicine, and the Book of Job," *Journal of Religion, Disability & Health* 16 (2012) 420–31.
17. M. Oeming and W. Drechsel, "Das Buch Hiob—ein Lehrstück der Seelsorge? Das Hiobbuch in exegetischer und poimenischer Perspektive," in *Das Buch Hiob und seine Interpetationen: Beiträge zum Hiob-Symposium auf dem Monte Verità vom 14.–19 August 2005* (ed. T. Krüger et al.; ATANT 88; Zurich: TVZ, 2007) 421–40.
18. K. Schmid, *Hiob als biblisches und antikes Buch: Historische und intellektuelle Kontexte seiner Theologie* (SBS 219; Stuttgart: Katholisches Bibelwerk, 2010).

on God's track record? How may we hold on to the goodness and loyalty of God in a world in which even the best human beings suffer? The
book of Job calls basic tenets of Israel's wisdom traditions into question.
The idea of a causal connection between action and consequence as the
foundation of ethics and cosmology crumbles under Job's criticism. *Creation theology* is another focus of the book: How should we understand
the realm of humans, of wild animals, of stars, the weather, and also the
underworld? *Social anthropology* is yet another focus of the book: What is
the relationship between the wisdom of old and young people (Elihu)? If
read as a *counseling guide*, the book of Job contains advice on how a wise
individual may deal with intense suffering. What may be the path back
to psychological and physical health? The answers given by the book are
intentionally complex.

9. *Who is the hero of the story; who is required to change?* In Christian
tradition as well as in most modern re-readings, *Job* himself is the "hero"
of the story. He is presented as an example to all who read the text (this
is especially true for the humble Job of the prose frame; see also James
5:11). *Jewish tradition* reads the text differently. There, *Job's friends* are
the heroes of the story, especially Elihu, because they are the defenders
of God himself. Job tends to be interpreted as an arrogant, blasphemous
foreigner. Several modern readings see the *satan* as the hero. His doubts
and inquisitive questioning, as well as his cruel tests, drive the plot forward. Some see *God* as the true hero of the narrative, either because God
risks encountering human beings, even though this might change him,
or rather because his love wins the day despite his unfathomable nature.
Who does the plot require to change? Does the author require *God* to learn
something?[19] Or is *Job* the rebel and the blasphemer who must radically
change his position?

It is difficult to discern who might be correct in this diverse scholarly
situation. Many literary and religious-historical questions (who? when?
where? to whom?) remain debated in current scholarship, even the question of theological content. The pulsating conflict of interpretations puts
everyone who engages in this scholarly discourse under its spell and pushes
each interpreter to formulate a personal response, especially because each
has undergone their own experiences with the sorrowful shadow of existence. We think that the divine answer according to the original intention

---

19. "Job is nothing more than an external opportunity for an intra-godly dispute"
(C. J. Jung, *Antwort an Hiob* [Olten: Walter, 1973] 24); "Yahweh's double nature has become clear, and someone or something had seen it and noticed. Such a revelation . . . could
not remain without consequences" (ibid., 32).

of the ancient author has a dialectical sharpening—on the one hand, a mortification that Job displays his small and marginal nature in the cosmos as well as the normality, even banality of suffering and death; on the other hand, an exaltation through which Job is valued and comforted so that God, who is limitlessly superior, turns to him and speaks with him. Nevertheless, it is quite clear that other interpreters also have good arguments and experiences. The conflict of interpretations is not, therefore, an expression of chaos and a lack of scholarly learning. They are inspired by the content and spur on toward still better argumentations. Neither the illusion of the best of all possible worlds nor the notion of a future world without suffering provides comfort, but only the acceptance of suffering.[20] We would like to invite each reader to undertake the journey through this book and to allow themselves to be caught up in the dynamic of bringing the story to life. The following essays on specific passages in the book of Job emphasize the path *that Job himself has to travel.* Job has a lot to learn! And Job takes the reader with him! We shall attempt to show that the book can be read as a whole. Its various sections display a high degree of sensitivity toward the human condition and thus provide us with much helpful material for counseling. It can be seen as a collection of "strategies of comfort":[21]

Various "Strategies of Comfort" in the Book of Job		
Person	*Type of Behavior*	*Texts*
Job comforts himself	a) stoic ataraxie	a) Job 1–2
	b) lament and disgust with one's existence	b) Job 3
	c) self-reassurance of one's own innocence	c) Job 31
	d) speaking of one's own suffering again and again	d) the dialogues 4–27
	e) hope (beyond death? vgl. Ps 49)	e) Job 19:25–29
	f) submission to God	f) Job 42:1–6
Job's wife	a) Intensification of desperation: "adiuvatrix diaboli"?	a) Job 2:9
	b) or: enabling lament and expression of suffering?	b) Job 2:9 esp. LXX

20. F. Lienhard, *Souffrance humaine et croix du Christ* (Lyon: Olivétan, 2006), esp. the sections "La passion des Job" (ibid., 30–35) and "La présence de Dieu au cœur du mal" (ibid., 76–79).

21. See Oeming and Drechsel, "Das Buch Hiob."

The three friends	a) silent presence b) listening c) critical reminders of previous tenets of faith d) emphasis on God's promises e) invitation to submit to God's will f) admonition to repentance	a) Job 2:12 b) Job 4:1–2 c) Job 4:3–4 d) Job 11:13, 17 e) Job 22:5–10
Elihu	a) pedagogy of suffering b) creation theology: God is good c) treasury of grace as God's ransom	a) Job 36, esp. vv .22–33 b) Job 37 c) Job 33:24–30
God	a) comfort through presence b) comfort through widening of horizons c) healthy disrespect	a) Job 38:1–2 b) Job 38:4–39:30 c) Job 40:6–32
The narrator	Narrative of encouragement about God's final restitution following all suffering. Emphasis on the reward for loyalty to God in prayer during times of temptation. Resurrection!	Job 42:6–17 (42:17 LXX)

Our thanks go to Joachim Vette (Heidelberg) and Peter Altmann (Zurich) who provided the English translation of the texts of this book, which is a revised and expanded version of Manfred Oeming and Konrad Schmid, *Hiobs Weg: Stationen von Menschen im Leid* (BTSt 45; Neukirchen-Vluyn, Neukirchener Verlag, 2001) and to Jim Eisenbraun from Eisenbrauns for taking care of the additional steps necessary for publication.

Abbreviations follow the *SBL Handbook of Style* (2nd ed.; Atlanta: SBL Press, 2014).

Manfred Oeming   Konrad Schmid

CHAPTER I

The Prologue to the Book of Job and the Problem of Job

KONRAD SCHMID

1. Introduction

As with all good literature, the Book of Job has successfully resisted interpretation, at least in regard to the fact that no interpretation has fully exhausted its potential meanings. It is not to be expected that this will change in the future.

It seems that the book of Job is inherently characterized by multi-dimensional perspectives that allow its readers to approach the book and the issues contained in it multiple times. It is thus no surprise that the actual topic of the book is still quite unclear. Does it deal with "unjust suffering," "theodicy," or "truth"? Edward Greenstein is probably correct when he writes: "Without in any way denying that the Book of Job examines a number of theological issues and human concerns, I have increasingly formed the impression that, even more than the book is about issues and themes, it is about the ways that we talk about them."[1]

Author's note: This text is based on the revised version of my contribution "Das Hiob-problem und der Hiobprolog," in: *Hiobs Weg: Stationen von Menschen im Leid* (M. Oeming and K. Schmid; Biblisch-Theologische Studien 45; Neukirchen-Vluyn: Neukirchener, 2001) 9–34, which was republished in K. Schmid, *Hiob als biblisches und antikes Buch: Die "Theologie" des Hiobbuchs in seinen innerbiblischen und kulturgeschichtlichen Kontexten* (SBS 219; Stuttgart: Katholisches Bibelwerk, 2010) 8–32.

1. E. Greenstein, "Truth or Theodicy? Speaking Truth to Power in the Book of Job," *Princeton Theological Seminary Bulletin* 27 (2006) 238–59; see also C. Newsom, *The Book of Job: A Contest of Moral Imaginations* (New York: Oxford University Press, 2003); I. Müll-ner, "Erkenntnis im Gespräch: Zur Bedeutung der (verbalen) Begegnung im Ijobbuch," in *Auf den Spuren der schriftgelehrten Weisen* (ed. I. Fischer et al.; BZAW 331; Berlin: de Gruyter 2003), 167–80; K. Engljähringer, *Theologie im Streitgespräch: Studien zur Dynamik der Dialoge des Buches Ijob* (SBS 198; Stuttgart: Katholisches Bibelwerk, 2003); G. Fischer,

Even the basic form of the book is characterized by a clear discursive structure—it contains mainly speeches—yet there are also further implicit discursive elements that fundamentally shape the theology of the book. The following feature is decisive: the separate sections—prologue, dialogues with the friends, the monologues of God, and the epilogue—can not only be characterized according to genre (and, as many assume, according to different stages of textual growth);[2] they also are engaged in a "conversation" that constitutes the very hermeneutical essence of the book.[3] How is the book understood, if we read it in light of the prologue?[4] How does it present itself, when we start with the epilogue?[5] What horizons are opened when we put the divine monologues at the center?[6] Such a plurality of reading strategies is not unusual for ancient forms of reading. Ancient texts, including biblical texts, were not simply read from beginning to end in order to gather the information contained in their pages; instead, they were well known as traditional texts used in scribal settings and read from various different vantage points.[7] Yet even modern readers, who "read through" the book of Job in its present order, can appreciate the interconnections and balancing act between the various sections. The memory of what has already been read sheds light on each new passage in the sequence of reading. Keeping all this in mind, we must consider the inner logic of the connections between the various parts: it is not possible to equate every position in the book with the intention of the author(s) of the book—at least where the connection between the narrative frame and the dialogues is concerned. We must also consider the possibility that God's final judgment in Job 42:7, which criticizes Job's friends and justifies Job himself, makes linear deductions impossible about certain redactional profiles that are based on specific statements in Job 3–27. With regard to its dramatic progression, the book of Job shares many similarities with *4 Ezra*, which may even have been influenced by the book of Job in its

"Heilendes Gespräch—Beobachtungen zur Kommunikation im Ijobbuch," in *Das Buch Ijob: Gesamtdeutungen—Einzeltexte—Zentrale Themen* (ed. T. Seidl and S. Ernst; ÖBS 31; Frankfurt a.M.: Lang, 2007) 184–200.

2. See below, section 2 (pp. 3ff.).

3. In this regard, the interpretation of A. Jepsen, *Das Buch Hiob und seine Deutung* (AzTh I/14; Stuttgart: Calwer, 1963), was way ahead of the exegesis of its time.

4. For example, Schmid, "Hiobproblem."

5. For example, K. N. Ngwa, *The Hermeneutics of the 'Happy' Ending in Job 42:7–17* (BZAW 345; Berlin: de Gruyter, 2005).

6. For example, O. Keel, *Jahwes Entgegnung an Ijob: Eine Deutung von Ijob 38–41 vor dem Hintergrund zeitgenössischer Bildkunst* (FRLANT 121; Göttingen: Vandenhoeck & Ruprecht, 1978).

7. K. van der Toorn, *Scribal Culture and the Making of the Hebrew Bible* (Cambridge: Harvard University Press, 2007) 75–108.

own final shape.[8] For *4 Ezra*, this shape has been emphasized considerably more than in the book of Job,[9] most likely due to the comparative consensus on its diachronic issues. Scholarship on the book of Job has not always seen with equal clarity that certain statements in the book depend on their specific literary position within the book and have their own intentional thrust. The following contribution will try to verify this hypothesis with special emphasis on the prologue of the book.

2. Introductory Issues Regarding the Literary Unity of the Book of Job

The fact that the book of Job—like almost all books of the Hebrew Bible—is a product of literary growth that includes its own oral prehistory can hardly be doubted simply on the basis of its transmission history. "*The*" book of Job does not exist. Already the Greek translation represents an updated edition of the book.[10] Ezek 14:14–20 seems to indicate an earlier—most likely oral—version of the subject matter when it mentions Job, Noah, and Daniel.[11]

---

8. F. García Martínez, "Traditions communes dans le IVe Esdras et dans les Mss de Qumran," *RdQ* 57–58 (1991) 287–301 (here 290); A. P. Hayman, "The Problem of Pseudonymity in the Ezra Apocalypse," *JSJ* (1975) 47–56 (here 56); M. A. Knibb, "Apocalyptic and Wisdom in 4 Ezra," *JSJ* 13 (1982) 56–74 (here 65–66); G. C. Macholz, "Die Entstehung des hebräischen Bibelkanons nach 4 Esra 14," in *Die Hebräische Bibel und ihre zweifache Nachgeschichte* (ed. E. Blum, G. C. Macholz, and E. W. Stegemann; Neukirchen-Vluyn: Neukirchener Verlag, 1990) 379–91 (here 380–81).

9. E. Brandenburger, *Die Verborgenheit Gottes im Weltgeschehen: Das literarische und theologische Problem des 4. Esrabuches* (ATANT 68; Zurich: TVZ, 1983) 30: "Was der Verfasser von IV Esra sagen will, läßt sich nicht aus einzelnen, aus dem Zusammenhang gerissenen Stellen belegen, vielmehr ist zur Ermittlung stets die bewegte und spannungsreiche Gedankenführung zu beachten"; W. Harnisch, "Der Prophet als Widerpart und Zeuge der Offenbarung: Erwägungen zur Interdependenz von Form und Sache im 4. Buch Esra," in *Apocalypticism in the Mediterranean World and the Near East* (ed. D. Hellholm; Tübingen: Mohr Siebeck, 1983) 461–93; idem, "Die Ironie der Offenbarung: Exegetische Erwägungen zur Zionvision im 4. Buch Esra," *ZAW* 95 (1983) 75–95; Schmid, "Esras Begegnung mit Zion: Die Deutung der Zerstörung Jerusalems im 4. Esrabuch und das Problem des 'bösen Herzens,'" *JSJ* 29 (1998) 261–77.

10. W. Dassmann, "Hiob," *RAC* 15: 366–442 (here 372–74); M. Witte, "The Greek Book of Job," in *Das Buch Hiob und seine Interpretationen: Beiträge zum Hiob-Symposium auf dem Monte Verità vom 14.–19. August 2005* (ed. T. Krüger et al.; ATANT 88; Zurich: TVZ, 2007) 33–54 ; C.-L. Seow, *Job 1–21: Interpretation and Commentary* (Illuminations; Grand Rapids: Eerdmans, 2013) 6–12.

11. M. Noth, "Noah, Daniel und Hiob in Ezechiel xiv," *VT* 1 (1951) 251–60; P. Weimar, "Literarkritisches zur Ijobnovelle," *BN* 12 (1980) 2–80 (here 80 n. 55); V. Maag, *Hiob: Wandlung und Verarbeitung des Problems in Novelle, Dialogdichtung und Spätfassungen* (FRLANT 128; Göttingen: Vandenhoeck & Ruprecht 1982) 45–49. See also H. M. Wahl, "Noah, Daniel und Hiob in Ezechiel XIV 12–20 (21–23): Anmerkungen zum traditionsgeschichtlichen Hintergrund," *VT* 42 (1992) 542–53; M. Köhlmoos, *Das*

It is, however, a matter of intense debate in current scholarship how the literary history of the book of Job should be reconstructed. A prominent hypothesis (presented in many different variations) separates the narrative prose frame from the much lengthier dialogues in the middle of the book (3:1 to 42:6).[12] Other debates focus on the issue of whether the scenes in heaven are an original part[13] of the prologue or secondary addition(s) to it.[14]

Auge Gottes: Textstrategie im Hiobbuch (FAT 25; Tübingen: Mohr Siebeck, 1999) 47 n. 3 (for bibliography), 49 n. 1; N. M. Sarna, "Epic Substratum in the Prose of Job," *JBL* 76 (1957) 13–25; critically N. C. Habel, *The Book of Job: A Commentary* (OTL; Philadelphia: Westminster 1985; here 35–36).

12. See, for example, F. Crüsemann's evaluation in "Hiob und Kohelet," in *Werden und Wirken des Alten Testaments* (ed. R. Albertz et al.; Göttingen: Vandenhoeck & Ruprecht, 1980) 373–93 (here 374 n. 7); for an overview of the history of scholarship, see M. Witte, *Vom Leiden zur Lehre: der dritte Redegang (Hiob 21–27) und die Redaktionsgeschichte des Hiobbuches* (BZAW 230; Berlin: de Gruyter, 1994) 36 n. 164, 192 n. 66.

13. J. Hempel, "Das theologische Problem des Hiob," in *Apoxysmata: Vorarbeiten zu einer Religionsgeschichte und Theologie des Alten Testaments* (ed. J. Hempel; Berlin: Töpelmann, 1961) 114–73 (with reference to the use of ברך in 1:5, 10, 11, 21; 2:5); G. Fohrer, "Zur Vorgeschichte und Komposition des Buches Hiob," *VT* 6 (1956) 249–67; repr. in *Studien zum Buche Hiob* (2nd ed.; ed. G. Fohrer; BZAW 159; Berlin: de Gruyter, 1983) 26–43; H. H. Schmid, *Wesen und Geschichte der Weisheit: Eine Untersuchung zur altorientalischen und israelitischen Weisheitsliteratur* (BZAW 101; Berlin: de Gruyter, 1966) 174 n. 148. A. Alt, "Zur Vorgeschichte des Buches Hiob," *ZAW* 14 (1937) 265–68; and Weimar, "Literarkritisches zur Ijobnovelle," 76 n. 4 assume that only one scene in heaven was part of the original narrative.

14. C. Kuhl, "Neuere Literarkritik des Buches Hiob," *TRu* 21 (1953) 163–205, 257–317 (here 196–97 n. 2); idem, "Vom Hiobbuche und seinen Problemen," *TRu* 22 (1954) 261–316 (here 295); F. Horst, *Hiob: 1. Teilband* (BK XVI/1; Neukirchen-Vluyn: Neukirchener Verlag, 1968) 4–5; L. Schmidt, *"De Deo": Studien zur Literarkritik und Theologie des Buches Jona, des Gesprächs zwischen Abraham und Jahwe in Gen 18,22ff und von Hi 1* (BZAW 143; Berlin: de Gruyter, 1976) 165–91; Crüsemann, "Hiob und Kohelet," 384 n. 6; R. Brandscheidt, *Gottes Zorn und Menschenleid: Die Gerichtsklage des leidenden Gerechten in Klgl 3* (TThSt 41; Trier: Paulinus-Verlag,1983) 294–302; H.-C. Schmitt, "Die Erzählung von der Versuchung Abrahams Gen 22,1–19* und das Problem einer Theologie der elohistischen Pentateuchtexte," *BN* 34 (1986) 82–109 (here 102 n. 98); J. Vermeylen, *Job, ses amis et son Dieu: La légende de Job et ses relectures postexiliques* (StB 2; Leiden: Brill, 1986) 8; L. Schwienhorst-Schönberger and G. Steins, "Zur Entstehung, Gestalt und Bedeutung der Ijob-Erzählung (Ijob 1f; 42)," *BZ* 33 (1989) 1–24; E. Kutsch, "Hiob und seine Freunde: Zu Problemen der Rahmenerzählung des Hiobbuches," in *Zur Aktualität des Alten Testaments* (ed. Siegfried Kreuzer and Kurt Lüthi; Frankfurt a.M.: Lang, 1992) 73–83; D. Fleming, "Job: The Tale of Patient Faith and the Book of God's Dilemma," *VT* 44 (1994) 468–82; O. Kaiser, *Grundriß der Einleitung in die kanonischen und deuterokanonischen Schriften des Alten Testaments* (3 vols.; Gütersloh: Gütersloher, 1994) 3:79 n. 5; U. Berges, "Der Ijobrahmen (Ijob 1,1–2,10; 42,7–17)," *BZ* 39 (1995) 225–45, (here 236–40 [further bibliography: 231 n. 21]); Köhlmoos, *Auge*, 50–51; H. Spieckermann, "Die Satanisierung Gottes: Zur inneren Konkordanz von Novelle, Dialog und Gottesreden im Hiobbuch," in *"Wer ist wie du, HERR, unter den Göttern?" Studien zur Theologie und Religionsgeschichte Israels* (ed. I. Kottsieper; Göttingen: Vandenhoeck & Ruprecht, 1994) 431–44 (here 433 n. 5); idem, "Hiob/Hiobbuch," pp. 1777–81 in *RGG.* 3:1778–79; M. Leuenberger, *Segen und*

Four arguments are usually mentioned to support the separation between the prose frame and the dialogues. First, (1) the difference between prose and poetry; (2) the use of the divine name YHWH[15] in the frame versus El,[16] Eloah,[17] Šadday,[18] and only rarely YHWH in the dialogues;[19] (3) the characterization of Job as a patient sufferer on the one hand and as an angry rebel on the other; and (4) the characterization of Job as a nomadic sheikh in the prose frame and as a well-to-do urbanite in the dialogues.[20]

Segenstheologien im alten Israel: Untersuchungen zu ihren religions- und theologiegeschichtlichen Konstellationen und Transformationen (ATANT 90; Zurich: TVZ, 2007) 421 n. 923.

The problematic fact that the 3mp suffixes in 1:13 refer back to the Job mentioned in 1:6–12 and also in 1:5 (see, however, the different reading in LXX) should not be emphasized too strongly. This may be no more than a stylistic device (see Weimar, "Literarkritisches zur Ijobnovelle," 76 n. 46); J. Ebach, *Streiten mit Gott—Hiob: Teil 1: 1–20* (5th ed.; Neukirchen-Vluyn: Neukirchener Verlag, 2013) 16, speaks of a "cross-fading technique" ("Überblendungstechnik").

W. Berg, "Gott und der Gerechte in der Rahmenerzählung des Buches Ijob," *Münchner Theologische Zeitschrift* 32 (1981) 205–21 (here 209 n. 15) remains undecided; see also the arguments presented in H.-P. Müller, *Das Hiobproblem: Seine Stellung und Entstehung im Alten Orient und im Alten Testament* (3rd ed.; EdF 84; Darmstadt: Wissenschaftliche Buchgesellschaft, 1995) 36–48, 183–86.

Mende presents a very idiosyncratic, extensively composition-critical reconstruction (T. Mende, *Durch Leiden zur Vollendung: Die Elihureden im Buch Ijob [Ijob 32–37]* [TThS 49; Trier: Paulinus-Verlag, 1990]; eadem, *Das Buch Ijob* [Düsseldorf: Patmos, 1993], see also L. Schwienhorst-Schönberger, "Ijob: Vier Modelle der Interpretation," in *Das Buch Ijob: Gesamtdeutungen—Einzeltexte—Zentrale Themen* [ed. T. Seidl and S. Ernst; ÖBS 31; Frankfurt a.M.: Lang, 2007] 21–38 [here 22–25]).

15. יהוה: Job 1:6, 7, 8, 9, 12, 21; 2:1, 2, 3, 4, 6, 7; 42:1, 7, 9, 10, 11, 12; אלהים: 1:1, 5, 6, 8, 9, 16, 22; 2:1, 3, 9, 10; 5:8; 20:29; 28:23; 32:2; 34:9; 38:7.

16. אל: 5:8; 8:3, 5, 13, 20; 9:2; 12:6; 13:3, 7, 8; 15:4, 11, 13, 25; 16:11; 18:21; 19:22; 20:15, 29; 21:14, 22; 22:2, 13, 17; 23:16; 25:4; 27:2, 9, 11, 13; 31:14, 23:28; 32:13; 33:4, 6, 14.29; 34:5.10, 12, 23, 31, 37; 35:2, 13; 36:5, 22, 26; 37:5, 10, 14; 38:41; 40:9, 19.

17. אלוה: 3:4, 23; 4:9, 17; 5:17; 6:4, 8, 9; 9:13; 10:2; 11:5, 6, 7; 12:4, 6; 15:8; 16:20, 21; 19:6, 21, 26; 21:9, 19; 22:12, 26; 24:12; 27:3, 8, 10; 29:2, 4; 31:2, 6; 33:12, 26; 35:10; 36:2; 37:15, 22; 39:17; 40:2.

18. שדי: 5:17; 6:4, 14; 8:3,5; 11:7; 13:3; 15:25; 21:15, 20; 22:3, 17, 23, 25, 26; 23:16; 24:1; 27:2, 10, 11, 13; 29:5; 31:2, 35; 32:8; 33:4; 34:10, 12; 35:13; 37:23; 40:2.

19. יהוה: 12:9; 38:1; 40:1, 6; אלהים: 5:8; 20:29; 28:23; 32:2; 34:9; 38:7.

20. A good overview is found in Kuhl, "Neuere Literarkritik," 186–98; Fohrer, "Zur Vorgeschichte"; R. Smend, *Die Entstehung des Alten Testaments* (Theologische Wissenschaft 1; Stuttgart: Kohlhammer, 1978) 202; Y. Hoffman, "The Relation between the Prologue and the Speech-Cycles in Job," *VT* 31 (1981) 160–70 (here 162); A. de Wilde, *Das Buch Hiob* (OTS 22; Leiden: Brill, 1981) 6; Vermeylen, *Job*, 3–7; J. Ebach, "Hiob/Hiobbuch," *TRE* 15:360–80 (here 363–64); Kaiser, *Grundriß*, 70–83; L. Schwienhorst-Schönberger, "Das Buch Ijob," in *Einleitung in das Alte Testament* (8th ed.; ed. Erich Zenger et al.; Stuttgart: Kohlhammer, 2004) 414–27 (here 420–23). Maag (*Hiob*, 10–19) attempts to construct an argument based on Job's origin in Uz, which for him indicates Aram, and that of the friends in an Edomite context. This argument remains unconvincing; cf. Kaiser, *Grundriß*, 80–81, as well as M. Görg, "Ijob aus dem Lande 'Zu," *BN* 12 (1980) 7–12; E. A. Knauf, "Supplementa Ismaelitica 4: Ijobs Heimat," *BN* 22 (1983) 25–29. On Job's illness

These observations, should they be correct, may well indicate two separate *sources* that first existed independently and were then woven together.[21] This assumption, however, leads to new problems. Scholars, especially in the 20th century, tended to argue as follows: "The following fact speaks against the assumption [. . .] that poetry and prose narrative were originally transmitted independently: The [chapters 3 to 42] are not imaginable without an introductory statement about Job's illness. The friends also have to be introduced somehow."[22]

The dialogues thus seem to be dependent on the frame as an introduction, at least with regard to its first part. Nevertheless, following the lead of Curt Kuhl ("Everything the reader needs to know in order to understand the book is contained in the monologues, i.e., Job 3, 29–31"),[23] an increasing number of scholars dispute this very fact.[24] An important element in this argument has been the reference to the so called "Babylonian Theodicy," as well as to *Ludlul bēl nēmeqi*.[25] In each case, the reader is provided with the necessary expositional material in the first-person speeches

in the prose frame and the dialogues, see Ebach, *Streiten*, 36; in regard to the בני בטני in Job 19:17, see Vermeylen, *Job*, 4.

21. Kaiser, *Grundriß*, 79; idem, *Der Gott des Alten Testaments*, Vol. 3 of *Theologie des Alten Testaments: Jahwes Gerechtigkeit* (UTB 2392; Göttingen: Vandenhoeck & Ruprecht, 2003) 269 accepts this conclusion.

22. L. Schmidt, *"De Deo,"* 171: "Gegen die Auffassung [. . .], daß Dichtung und Rahmenerzählung ursprünglich getrennt überliefert wurden, spricht die Tatsache, daß [die Kapitel 3 bis 42] ohne eine einleitende Bemerkung, daß Hiob krank war, nicht vorstellbar [sind]. Auch die Freunde müssen in irgendeiner Weise eingeführt werden." See Spieckermann, "Hiob/Hiobbuch," 1778; A. Scherer, *Lästiger Trost: Ein Gang durch die Eliphas-Reden im Hiobbuch* (BTSt 98: Neukirchen-Vluyn: Neukirchener Verlag, 2008) 6–7 n. 9.

23. Kuhl, "Neuere Literarkritik," 194: "alles, was der Leser zum Verständnis braucht, [ist] in den Monologen [sc. Hi 3.29–31] gesagt."

24. See Witte, *Leiden*, 192 n. 66; idem, "Review of Melanie Köhlmoos, *Das Auge Gottes*," *TLZ* 159 (2000) 885–88 (here 888); Kaiser, *Gott*, 272; W.-D. Syring, *Hiob und sein Anwalt: Die Prosatexte des Hiobbuches und ihre Rolle in seiner Redaktions- und Rezeptionsgeschichte* (BZAW 336; Berlin: de Gruyter, 2004) 127, 169; J. van Oorschot, "Die Entstehung des Hiobbuches," in *Das Buch Hiob und seine Interpretationen: Beiträge zum Hiob-Symposium auf dem Monte Verità vom 14.–19. August 2005* (ed. T. Krüger et al.; ATANT 88; Zurich: TVZ, 2007) 165–84 (here 169–74); K.-J. Illman, "Theodicy in Job," in *Theodicy in the World of the Bible* (ed. A. Laato and J. C. de Moor; Leiden: Brill, 2003) 305–33 (here 314; see however 306); Leuenberger, *Segen*, 419–20; see C. Newsom, "Considering Job," *CRB* 1 (1993) 87–118 (here 160).

25. See A. Annus and A. Lenzi, *Ludlul bēl nēmeqi: The Standard Babylonian Poem of the Righteous Sufferer* (SAA 7; Publications of the Foundation for Finnish Assyriological Research 2. Helsinki: The Neo-Assyrian Text Corpus Project, 2010), see in greater detail F. Sedlmaier, "Ijob und die Auseinandersetzungsliteratur im alten Mesopotamien," in *Das Buch Ijob: Gesamtdeutungen—Einzeltexte—Zentrale Themen* (ed. T. Seidl and S. Ernst; ÖBS 31; Frankfurt a.M.: Lang, 2007) 85–136 ; C. Uehlinger, "Das Hiob-Buch im Kontext der altorientalischen Literatur- und Religionsgeschichte," in *Das Buch Hiob und seine Inter-*

and the dialogues: "In the context of ancient Near Eastern literature it is thus quite possible to imagine the Job dialogues without their narrative frame; this may not even be unusual, even if our present reading habits suggest otherwise."[26] Yet, it still remains an open question whether these examples are truly relevant, as they show a much lesser degree of complexity in regard to content and characters than the book of Job.

In the case of the "Babylonian Theodicy" we only encounter a *two-person dialogue*—a communicative setting easily understood even without a scenic introduction. In addition, the 27 verses are shaped as an acrostic; 11 verses all begin the same, thus clearly identifying one speaker, who presents himself simultaneously as the author: *a-na-ku sa-ag-gi-il-ki-[i-na-am-u]b-bi-ib ma-áš-ma-šu ka-ri-bu ša i-li ú šar-ri* "I, Sangil-kinamubbib, the conjuror, who blesses and greets god and the king."[27]

Ludlul bēl nēmeqi is a text on four tablets framed by a hymn (I.1–40; IV.99–120). It probably consists of 120 lines, the central section consisting of the lament of a suffering individual (I.41–III.8) and the report of his convalescence (III.9–IV.98).[28] This text presents just a single speaker.

As we can see, the parallels are remarkable, but it remains an open question whether they can adequately support the existence of a Job poem without narrative exposition. We also must consider the problem that we cannot reconstruct an original beginning for the Job poem based on Job 3. Based on the narrative introductions to the later speeches of the friends (Job 4:1; 6:1 etc.), we cannot assume that the onset of the direct speech in Job 3:3 is the beginning of the Job poem. The verses Job 3:1–2, however, are so clearly shaped as a transition from Job 1–2 to Job 3–27 that they

---

pretationen: Beiträge zum Hiob-Symposium auf dem Monte Verità vom 19.–23.8.2005 (ed. T. Krüger et al.; ATANT 88; Zurich: TVZ, 2007) 97–162.

26. Van Oorschot, "Entstehung," 174: "In . . . beiden Fällen entnimmt der Leser die Exposition von Inhalt und redenden Personen der 'Ich'-Rede bzw. dem Dialog selbst. Eine Hiobdichtung ohne Rahmen ist also im Kontext der altorientalischen Literatur sehr wohl denkbar und, anders als unsere Lesegewohnheiten es uns suggerieren wollen, keineswegs ungewöhnlich." See also U. Nõmmik, *Die Freundesreden des ursprünglichen Hiobdialogs: Eine form- und traditionsgeschichtliche Studie* (BZAW 410; Berlin: de Gruyter, 2010) 279, 299.

27. W. G. Lambert, *Babylonian Wisdom Literature* (Oxford: Oxford University Press, 1960; repr. Winona Lake, IN: Eisenbrauns, 1996), 63; *TUAT* III, 143; see C. Uehlinger, "Hiob-Buch," 147; Sedlmaier, "Ijob," 118.

28. H. Spieckermann, "*Ludlul bēl nēmeqi* und die Frage nach der Gerechtigkeit Gottes," in *Gottes Liebe zu Israel: Studien zur Theologie des Alten Testaments* (ed. H. Spieckermann; FAT 33; Tübingen: Mohr Siebeck 2001) 103–18 (here 105–6); see R. Albertz, "*Ludlul bēl nēmeqi*—eine Lehrdichtung zur Ausbreitung und Vertiefung der persönlichen Mardukfrömmigkeit," in *Geschichte und Theologie: Studien zur Exegese des Alten Testaments und zur Religionsgeschichte Israels* (BZAW 326; Berlin: de Gruyter, 2003) 85–105.

must be excluded as an original beginning.[29] Yet without the reconstruction of an original beginning, the assumption of an independent Job poem is not plausible in and of itself.

Whether or not the narrative frame itself can be considered self-sufficient is not an easy question. It is, in any case, much less obvious than many tend to assume. Some scholars do believe that the prologue and the epilogue (often without the scenes in heaven[30] and thus—due to the close connections to these scenes—chapter two as a whole) can be joined together, resulting in a succinct and complete Job narrative. This narrative would then consist of 1:1–5, 13–21 (22) + 42:11–16/17.[31] This collection of verses indeed produces a fairly coherent narrative, yet it remains strangely trite. Such a story presents a hero who is made to suffer, remains steadfast in his suffering, and is then richly rewarded. As a diachronic argument, scholars often point to the fact that a redactional break can be recognized after 42:7–10, which precedes the ending in 42:11–17. The latter makes no mention of the friends. It is not a foregone conclusion, however, that 42:10 and 42:11–17 contradict each other. Job's restitution, which takes place over a period of time, is announced in 42:10 as a superscription[32] and then unfolds in 42:11–17. The absence of the friends[33] in 42:11–17 is not really an issue, as they are bid farewell in 42:9. Given the development of the plot, the assumption that the visit by the friends stands in "competition"[34] with the visit by the siblings and neighbors is also not immediately compelling. Even observations such as the fact that Job's illness is no longer mentioned in the epilogue fail to qualify as stringent indicators of a diachronic break.

---

29. Cf. K. Schmid, "Innerbiblische Schriftauslegung: Aspekte der Forschungsgeschichte," in *Schriftauslegung in der Schrift* (ed. R. G. Kratz, T. Krüger, and K. Schmid; BZAW 300; Berlin: de Gruyter, 2000) 1–22.

30. Cf. above, nn. 13–14.

31. See the classic presentation by Alt, "Zur Vorgeschichte des Buches Hiob" (Job 1:1–22; 42:11–17; on the history of scholarship as a whole, see Syring, *Hiob und sein Anwalt*, 7–50); more recently, Spieckermann, "Satanisierung," 433; Syring, *Hiob und sein Anwalt*, 154–58 (Job 1:1–3*, 13–21*, 42:11*, 12b–13?); T. Krüger, "Das Buch Hiob," in *Erklärt: Der Kommentar zur Zürcher Bibel* (ed. M. Krieg and K. Schmid; Zurich: TVZ 2009) 2:1098–1147 (Job 1:1–5, 13–21[, 22] + 42:11–16); Leuenberger, *Segen*, 421 n. 923; see also ibid., 443–44, for an attractive interpretation of this narrative.

32. For a critical but somewhat mechanical view of the superscription in 42:10, see Schwienhorst-Schönberger and Steins, "Zur Entstehung, Gestalt und Bedeutung der Ijob-Erzählung," 10.

33. "[D]aß nicht auch noch Hiobs Frau (2,9f) und der Satan (1,6ff.; 2,1ff.) ausdrücklich abgefertigt werden, ist nur ein Gewinn" (Alt, "Zur Vorgeschichte des Buches Hiob," 267). (The fact that Job's wife and the *satan* are not also explicitly dealt with can only be seen positively.)

34. Van Oorschot, "Die Entstehung des Hiobbuches," 167.

A further observation points to the fact that a clearly recognizable structure is missing from this reconstructed narrative: it consists only of a prologue and an epilogue. Such a structure, however, should be expected if we take the strict formulaic language of these passages seriously. From this perspective, Maag's[35] proposal of an original third scene in heaven, placed between 2:10 and 42:11 and thus completing the alternation between heaven and earth, makes sense—although this proposal has no other argument in its favor.

Whoever intends to join prologue and epilogue together as an originally independent narrative can only do so at severe cost to its theological value. This cost is increased further by eliminating the scenes in heaven. Ever since Wellhausen, it has become customary to excuse this "simplicity" by referring to its origin in the context of an unrefined collection of "folk tales."[36] The narrative thus presents us not with theology but with folklore in its most rudimentary form.

This is nothing more than a stopgap solution, which we should not accept unless there truly is no alternative. Without intending to trivialize the literary problem of the book of Job, we can nevertheless argue for the assumption of a *substantial* interconnection between frame and dialogues—even when allowing for the fact that each has undergone its

35. Maag, *Hiob*, 37–41. Alt, "Zur Vorgeschichte des Buches Hiob," 267 also assumes missing text in his reconstructed narrative (Job 1:1–2:13 . . . 42:7–10): "An important but probably short section of text is missing from this version of the narrative: the spelling out of Job's disagreement with his friends, which God decided in Job 42:7–8 in Job's favor" ["verloren aus dieser Fassung der Erzählung [ist] allerdings ein sehr wichtiges, wenn auch wahrscheinlich nicht umfangreiches Stück: der Wortlaut von Hiobs Streit mit den Freunden, den Jahwe in 42,7f zu Hiobs Gunsten entscheidet"]. We can only reconstruct a prior version consisting of Job 1; 42:11–17 from the present text.

36. See J. Wellhausen, "Review of August Dillmann, *Hiob*," *JDT* 16 (1871) 552–57, (here 555); B. Duhm, *Das Buch Hiob* (KHC XVI; Freiburg: Mohr [Siebeck], 1897) vii–viii, 1; K. Budde, *Das Buch Hiob* (HK II/1; Göttingen: Vandenhoeck & Ruprecht, 1913) xi–xiv (see also the survey in J. Gray, "The Book of Job in the Context of Near Eastern Literature," *ZAW* 82 (1970) 251–69 (here 265 n. 35); Syring, Hiob *und sein Anwalt*, 33–34); see the discussion in Kuhl, "Neuere Literarkritik," 191–93; H. Gese, *Lehre und Wirklichkeit in der alten Weisheit: Studien zu den Sprüchen Salomos und zu dem Buche Hiob* (Tübingen: Mohr Siebeck, 1958), 71; J. Crenshaw, "Job, Book of," *ABD* 3:858–68 (here 863); P. Ritter-Müller, *Kennst du die Welt? Gottes Antwort an Ijob: Eine sprachwissenschaftliche und exegetische Studie zur ersten Gottesrede Ijob 38 und 39* (Altes Testament und Moderne 5; Münster: LIT, 2000), 19; with regard to an English speaking context, see also the list in R. D. Moore, "The Integrity of Job," *CBQ* 45 (1983) 17–31 (here 17–18 n. 2). Critical voices against the assumption of a "collection of folk tales" are found with Hempel, "Das theologische Problem des Hiob," 131–38; M. Buber, *Der Glaube der Propheten* (Zurich: Manesse, 1950) 271; Schmid, *Wesen und Geschichte der Weisheit*, 174; Moore, "The Integrity of Job"; R. N. Whybray, *Job: Readings* (Sheffield: Sheffield Academic Press, 1998) 14; see also Spieckermann, "Hiob/Hiobbuch," 1779. Arguments for the dating of the prose frame are also relevant for this issue.

own diachronic development, including earlier oral stages. This is also not a new suggestion.[37] We can also refer to the Ahiqar novel, which gives no indication of textual growth; it, too, places a prose frame around wisdom poetry.[38]

As an alternative to a general separation between frame and dialogues, we can thus examine whether the above-mentioned textual oddities can also be explained by the course of the narrative itself; this is indeed quite possible. The change of Job from a passive sufferer to a rebel, a fact that has been seen as a weighty argument for diachronic separation, is part of a dramatic development that in and of itself does not call the coherence of the text into question.[39] Job simply starts passively and then turns into a rebel.[40] The same is true for the difference between the prose texts in the frame and the poetry in the dialogues: they should be explained in terms

---

37. The following scholars had already questioned the literary-critical separation between frame and dialogues: G. Hölscher, *Das Buch Hiob* (HAT I/17; Tübingen: Mohr Siebeck, 1952) 4–5; H. H. Rowley, "The Book of Job and Its Meaning," *BJRL* 41 (1958/1959) 167–207 (here 184), and see also those mentioned p. 177 n. 3; more recently, Habel, *Book of Job*; idem, "The Narrative Art of Job: Applying the Principles of Robert Alter," *JSOT* 27 (1983) 101–11 (with important observations on thematic and semantic connections between the frame and the dialogues); J. Hartley, *The Book of Job* (NICOT; Grand Rapids: Eerdmans, 1988); de Wilde, *Das Buch Hiob*, 8; Hoffman, "The Relation between the Prologue and the Speech-Cycles in Job"; idem, "Ancient Near Eastern Literary Conventions and the Restoration of the Book of Job," *ZAW* 103 (1991) 399–411 (for a differentiated position, see idem, *A Blemished Perfection: The Book of Job in Context* [JSOTSup 213; Sheffield: Sheffield Academic Press, 1996] 299); Moore, "The Integrity of Job"; Whybray, *Job*, 11–12; H.-P. Mathys, Zum literarischen Charakter des Hiobbuches," in *Das Buch Hiob: Dichtung als Theologie* (ed. G. Kaiser and H.-P. Mathys; BTSt 81; Neukirchen-Vluyn: Neukirchener Verlag, 2006) 123–29; Seow, *Job 1–21*, 26–38; see also the discussion in Müller, *Das Hiobproblem*, 36–48 as well as Keel, *Jahwes Entgegnung*, 158 n. 427. Note also the trend mentioned in J. van Oorschot, "Tendenzen der Hiobforschung," *TRu* 59 (1994) 352–88 (here, 356): "Dabei nimmt die Zahl der Exegeten zu, die hinter den Prosa- und Poesieteilen *eine* gestaltende Hand erkennen." This evaluation coheres with the position of W. A. M. Beuken ("Introduction," in *The Book of Job* [ed. W. A. M. Beuken; BETL 114; Leuven: Peeters, 1994] i–viii, [here, vii]): "1. Literary-historical criticism no longer leads to the theory of different origins for the framework in prose and the poetic corpus of the book of Job. 2. Redaction-historical criticism is fruitfully concentrating upon specific segments of the book of Job, such as the speeches of Elihu, some parts of the dialogue between Job and the friends, chapter 28, the two speeches of God and the two replies of Job." See also the comments by C. Newsom, "Re-considering Job," CBR 5 (2007) 155–82 (here 161).

38. H. Niehr, *Aramaic Ahiqar* (*JSHRZ* II/2; Gütersloh: Gütersloher, 2007) see H.-P. Müller, "Die Hiobrahmenerzählung und ihre alt-orientalischen Parallelen als Paradigmen einer weisheitlichen Wirklichkeitswahrnahme," in *The Book of Job* (ed. W. A. M. Beuken; BETL 114; Leuven: Peeters, 1994) 21–39 (here 28–30); E. A. Knauf and P. Guillaume, "Job," in *Introduction à l'Ancien Testament* (ed. T. Römer; MoBi 49; Geneva: Labor et Fides, 2004) 501–10 (here 505).

39. See Crenshaw, "Job, Book of," 860; Ebach, *Streiten*, 1; Maag, *Hiob*, 106.

40. See the observations on the connections between Job 3–27 and Job 1–2 in R. W. E. Forrest, "The Two Faces of Job: Imagery and Integrity in the Prologue," in *Ascribe to the*

of a change in genre, not as the result of textual growth[41]—as can be seen in the fact that Job's speeches in the prologue are poetry and the introductions to the speeches in the dialogues are prose.

The alternation between prose narrative and poetic speech is also connected to the varying use of the divine name.[42] The fact that the poetic passages tend to use El (אל), Eloah (אלוה), or Šaddai (שׁדי) compared to a dominant use of Yhwh (יהוה) in the prose sections is not really remarkable. Its supposed indicative strength is further diminished by the fact that the narrative introductions to the individual speeches throughout the book all use YHWH. What remains as an argument is the observation that Job appears as a nomadic sheikh versus an urbanite. This observation alone holds little value because neither the frame nor the dialogues describe Job's precise social context with any detail.

These thoughts should not lead us to assume the literary unity of the book of Job as a whole. At the very least, we should note that Job 28,[43] as well as the Elihu speeches (Job 32–37), which may have enabled the book to be included in the canon,[44] are secondary additions. Other passages

---

Lord: Biblical and Other Studies in Memory of P. C. Craigie (ed. Lyle Eslinger and G. Taylor; JSOTSup 67; Sheffield: Sheffield Academic Press, 1988) 385–98.

41. See Kuhl, "Neuere Literarkritik," 188.

42. See de Wilde, *Buch Hiob,* 4.

43. Formally, the "song of wisdom" is a monologue by Job that at least in part fulfills the function of showing that Job did not fully reject all of the "wise" explanations presented by the friends. On Job 28, see J. van Oorschot, "Hiob 28: Die verborgene Weisheit und die Furcht Gottes als Überwindung einer generalisierten חכמה," in *The Book of Job* (ed. W. A. M. Beuken; BETL 114; Leuven: Peeters, 1994) 183–201; A. Lo, *Job 28 as Rhetoric: An Analysis of Job 28 in the Context of Job 22–31* (VTSup 97; Leiden: Brill, 2003); S. C. Jones, *Rumors of Wisdom: Job 28 as Poetry* (BZAW 398; Berlin: de Gruyter, 2009), as well as the collection of articles in E. van Wolde, ed., *Job 28: Cognition in Context* (BIS 64; Leiden: Brill, 2003). I. Müllner, "Der Ort des Verstehens: Ijob 28 als Teil der Erkenntnisdiskussion des Ijobbuches," in *Das Buch Ijob: Gesamtdeutungen—Einzeltexte—Zentrale Themen* (ed. T. Seidl and S. Ernst; ÖBS 31; Frankfurt a.M.: Lang, 2007) 57–83 (here 62–63), presents a helpful survey of scholarship.

44. Even though Elihu does not really say anything substantially new (see Witte, *Hiobbuch,* 425), his statements do not fall under the divine verdict in Job 42:7. With regard to Elihu's monologues, see Wahl, *Schöpfer*; M. Witte, "Noch einmal: Seit wann gelten die Elihureden im Hiobbuch (Kap. 32–37) als Einschub?" *BN* 67 (1993) 20–25; Kaiser, *Grundriß*, 75–76; idem, *Gott*, 279–82; Köhlmoos, *Auge*, 62–63; Vermeylen, *Créateur*; T. Pilger, *Erziehung im Leiden: Komposition und Theologie der Elihureden in Hiob 32–37* (FAT II/49; Tübingen: Mohr Siebeck, 2010), with a highly differentiated redaction-critical approach; also E. A. Knauf, "Hiobs Heimat," *WO* 19 (1988) 65–83 (here 67): "Es handelt sich bei den Elihureden wahrscheinlich um den ersten orthodoxen Kommentar zu diesem ganz heterodoxen Buch, der dessen Aufnahme in den Kanon möglich gemacht hat." On chapters 32 to 37 as a commentary, see also C. Newsom, *The Book of Job: A Contest of Moral Imaginations* (New York: Oxford University Press, 2003) 200–233; I. Müllner, "Literarische Diachronie in den Elihureden des Ijobbuches (Ijob 32–37)," in *Das Manna fällt auch heute noch: Beiträge zur Geschichte und Theologie des Alten, Ersten Testaments* (ed. F.-L. Hossfeld and L.

throughout the book also appear as editorial supplements.[45] Nevertheless, the reservations against the classic diachronic hypothesis separating the frame and the dialogues (and postulating an original short Job novel and Job poem) are large enough that this assumption should no longer form the foundation of Job interpretation.[46] The hypothesis of a "collection of folk tales" is especially problematic. I believe it more plausible to postulate a narrative frame dependent on the dialogues—be it as a secondary interpretation or as their original pre- and postlude.

3. The Hermeneutical Problem of the Prologue to the Book of Job

Within the Bible, the prologue of the book of the Job stands apart as something unique. Those who read this text cannot quite shake the impression that they are being told a fairy tale. This not only involves the beginning איש היה בארץ עוץ "There was a man in the land of Uz" (Job 1:1), to which we may automatically want to add: "Once upon a time." It also, or especially, involves the two scenes in heaven that allow a fairy-tale-like insight into heaven itself. God and the *satan*[47]—the text refers to a lower

---

Schwienhorst-Schönberger; Herders Biblische Studien 44; Freiburg: Herder 2004) 447–69. D. J. A. Clines ("The Fear of the Lord is Wisdom" (Job 28:28): A Semantic and Contextual Study," in *Job 28: Cognition in Context* [ed. E. van Wolde; BIS 64; Leiden: Brill, 2003] 57–92; idem, "Putting Elihu in his Place: A Proposal for the Relocation of Job 32–37," *JSOT* 29 [2004] 243–53) and E. Greenstein ("The Poem of Wisdom in Job 28 in its Conceptual and Literary Contexts," in *Job 28: Cognition in Context* [ed. E. van Wolde; BIS 64; Leiden: Brill, 2003] 253–80) understand Job 28 und Job 32–37 to be closely connected and assume a reordering of the text that led to the current sequence of chapters. The rabbinic interpretation values the Elihu passages very highly; see Dassmann, "Hiob," 371.

45. Based on the Ptolemaic-Egyptian imagery (instead of the ancient Near Eastern images in the first monologue), Uehlinger ("Hiob-Buch," 122) believes the second divine monologue to be a secondary addition. Compare Spieckermann, "Hiob/Hiobbuch," 1781.

46. This essay cannot deal adequately with the detailed diachronic arguments regarding the book of Job proposed by Witte (*Vom Leiden zur Lehre*; compare his summary in "Das Hiobbuch," in *Grundinformation Altes Testament* (4th ed.; ed. J. C. Gertz; UTB 2745; Göttingen: Vandenhoeck & Ruprecht, 2010] 432–45); and R. M. Wanke, *Praesentia Dei: Die Vorstellungen von der Gegenwart Gottes im Hiobbuch* (BZAW 421; Berlin: de Gruyter, 2013).

47. On the figure of *satan*, see Kuhl, "Neuere Literarkritik," 195–98; J. Lévêque, *Job et son Dieu : Volume I: Essai d'exégèse et de théologie biblique* (EtB; Paris: Librairie Lecoffre, 1970) 179–90; Maag, *Hiob*, 63–75; P. L. Day, *An Adversary in Heaven: śaṭan in the Hebrew Bible* (HSM 43; Atlanta: Scholars, 1988); D. J. A. Clines, *Job 1–20* (WBC 17; Dallas: Word, 1989) 19–23 (and bibliography); V. P. Hamilton, "Satan," *ABD* 5: 985–89; K. Nielsen, "שׂטן" *TWAT* 7:745–51 (bibliography on 746); C. Breytenbach and P. L. Day, "Satan," *DDD*: 1369–80; M. Gies and O. Böcher, "Satan," in *Neues Bibel-Lexikon* (Zurich: Benziger, 1999) 12/13: 448–52; H. A. Kelly, *Satan: A Biography* (Cambridge: Cambridge University Press, 2006). On the heavenly court, see M. E. Polley, "Hebrew Prophecy Within the Council of Yahweh: Examined in its ANE Setting," pp. 141–56 in *Scripture in Context: Essays*

minion of heaven—work out a deal over the fate of Job,[48] and the readers can observe their conversation as if they were in heaven themselves.

Is it proper to speak of God as the prologue does? What is the purpose of speaking about God in this manner? Is this not merely talk *of* God, talk *about* God as Bultmann has defined it[49]—a manner of speaking that turns God into an object, makes him a thing in heaven?

In order to deal with ancient texts such as the prologue of the book of Job, scholars tend to refer to ancient cosmology that imagines a heavenly sphere existing above the earthly realm. The heavenly sphere can be the setting for actions and events just like the earth below. Although this perspective is certainly true, its relevance is limited. The limits lie where the reference to ancient cosmology leads to a cessation of interpretation. It does not suffice to explain the scene in heaven as merely the result of ancient cosmology and then pay no further attention to it.

We should instead emphasize one methodological and one historical factor. In terms of method, we should prefer any thematically plausible explanation of the particular shape of the prologue to other alternatives that merely explain it as the result of the contemporary worldview. On a historical level, we need to consider the fact that the seemingly archaic view of heaven in the prologue does not necessarily match the supposed postexilic date of the text.[50] This worldview is not self-evident confirmation of such a time-frame.

---

on the Comparative Method (ed. C. A. Evans et al.; PTMS 34; Pittsburgh: Pickwick 1980) 141–56; G. Fohrer, *Das Buch Hiob* (2nd ed.; KAT 16; Gütersloh: Gütersloher, 1986) 80–81 (and bibliography); H.-J. Fabry, "סוד," *TWAT* 5:775–82; H. D. Preuss, *Einführung in die alttestamentliche Weisheitsliteratur* (UB 383; Stuttgart: Kohlhammer, 1987) 104–7; E. T. Mullen Jr., *The Assembly of the Gods: The Divine Council in Canaanite and Early Hebrew Literature* (HSM 24; Atlanta: Scholars, 1980); idem, "Divine Assembly," *ABD* 2:214–17; L. K. Handy, "The Authorization of Divine Power and the Guilt of God in the Book of Job: Useful Ugaritic Parallels," *JSOT* 60 (1993) 107–18; H.-D. Neef, *Gottes himmlischer Thronrat: Hintergrund und Bedeutung von sôd JHWH im Alten Testament* (AzTh 79; Stuttgart: Calwer, 1994) (see also the bibliography in S. Parpola, *Assyrian Prophecies* [SAA 9; Helsinki: Helsinki University Press, 1997] lxxxiii).

48. "So ganz auf Du und Du" (Wellhausen, "Review of August Dillmann, *Hiob*," 555).

49. See R. Bultmann, "Welchen Sinn hat es, von Gott zu reden?" in *Glauben und Verstehen: Gesammelte Aufsätze* (3rd ed.; Tübingen: Mohr Siebeck, 1958) 1:26–37.

50. See A. Hurvitz, "The Date of the Prose-Tale of Job Linguistically Reconsidered," *HTR* 67 (1974) 17–34; Witte, *Vom Leiden zur Lehre*, 192 n. 63 (bibliography); see also E. Blum, *Die Komposition der Vätergeschichte* (WMANT 57; Neukirchen-Vluyn: Neukirchener Verlag, 1984), 329 with n. 112 (bibliography); Kaiser, *Grundriß*, 78–79, as well as K. Schmid, "The Authors of the Book of Job and the Problem of their Historical and Social Settings," in *Sages, Scribes, and Seers: Wise Men and Women in the Eastern Mediterranean World* (ed. L. G. Perdue; FRLANT 219; Göttingen: Vandenhoeck & Ruprecht 2008), 145–53.

The first impression of the prologue as a naive fairly tale about heaven
may thus be a deception. As a matter of fact, we can recognize a clear
theological intention behind the conspicuous shape of the prologue, an
intention that only becomes clear when we look closely at the text within
its larger context.

4. *The Interpretation of the Book of Job*
through the Lens of the Prologue

Based on the reflections on the textual growth of the book of Job presented above, one thing should have become clear: when we deal with the
prologue to the book of Job, there is *no obvious reason* why we should read
it solely in isolation or in connection with the epilogue at the end of the
book; instead, we should interpret it within the context of the *book of Job as
a whole*. In term of its literary history, it seems that the prologue never was
anything but a *prologue*; there probably never was a Job text that consisted
only of the narrative frame (1:1–22 + 42:11–17 or parts thereof), be it
with or without the scenes in heaven. In this, those that believe the prose
sections were composed as a redactional frame for the dialogues agree with
those who assume an original text containing both prose and dialogues.
However, those who continue to advocate for the existence of an ancient
Job folk tale can apply the following comments to the secondary redactional interweaving of the frame and the dialogues.

When we interpret the prologue within the context of the rest of the
book, we realize quickly that the prologue contains important theological
statements with regard to the book as a whole. The most important statement, which we must mention first of all, is: *the prologue provides not only
an exposition of the problem of the book of Job but also presents its solution.*[51]
The first two chapters not only describe the circumstances of Job's suffering; they also provide the reason behind it.

We must see this with utmost clarity: according to the prologue, Job's
suffering has a very simple, not to say a grotesquely simplistic, explanation:
Job is subjected to a heavenly test.[52] This is the only reason for his suffer-

---

51. See Gese, *Lehre und Wirklichkeit in der alten Weisheit*, 71: "Das Problem un-
gerechtfertigt erscheinenden Leidens scheint im Prolog theoretisch gelöst zu sein." I believe
that Ebach (*Streiten*, 12) discards the prologue too early: "Es geht um die Frage, wie es
um Hiobs Frömmigkeit und Gottes Gerechtigkeit steht, nicht um die Frage, ob Gott oder
der Satan sich durchsetzen wird. Das ist der Grund dafür, daß die Himmelsszenen (1,6–12;
2,1–7) zwar zur Exposition des Hiobproblems erforderlich sind, an keiner Stelle des Buches
jedoch als 'Lösung' dieses Problems aufgeboten werden."
52. We can state with Horst (*Hiob*, 16) that this should not be understood as a bet—as
Job 1–2 was often understood through the influence of Goethe's *Faust* (see Ebach, *Streiten*,

ing. God performs a cruel experiment on Job;[53] despite the figure of the *satan*, it is he who is solely responsible for Job's fate (compare 1:11 with 1:12; 2:3; see also 1:21; 2:10). The text is especially careful to show that each of the *satan*'s actions affecting Job is legitimized and limited by God. In 2:3, God himself admits that it was not the *satan* who destroyed Job, but that the *satan* drove God to act against Job (סות *Hiphil*).[54]

There is one modification we must immediately make to this proleptic solution to the problem of Job: neither Job *himself* nor are his wife or friends aware of this solution. Job only knew his suffering, not the book that carries his name. The readers alone have knowledge of the true reason for the blows that befell Job; and they have been aware of this reason from the very beginning, from chapter one.

The argument that the prologue solves the problem of Job at the very beginning of the book is not new. Wellhausen had already pointed this out and wondered, in reference to the prologue, whether it could be good narrative strategy to reveal the solution to the problem at the same time when the problem was presented.[55] All of the following chapters from Job 3:1 to 42:6 circle around this very question: why must Job suffer? So why reveal the answer to this question already at the beginning of the book?

14–15): "Wenn es auch um die Feststellung der Wahrheit einer Behauptung geht, so fehlt doch das Strafgedinge für den Fall, daß die Behauptung sich als unwahr erweist. Demzufolge spielt dann auch der Satan im Epilog keine Rolle mehr." See also R. N. Whybray, "The Immorality of God: Reflections on Some Passages in Genesis, Job, Exodus and Numbers," *JSOT* 72 (1996) 89–120 (here 108–9): "Satan's absence from the epilogue confirms that Yahweh has been solely responsible for what has been done."

53. See also Lévêque, *Job et son Dieu*, 192–230; Handy, "The Authorization of Divine Power." Compare the reference to the Targum that paraphrases 1:12 and 2:7: "And the *satan* left with the permission (בהרמנא) of YHWH."

54. On this, see *HALAT* 3:707.

55. ". . . dem Leser von vornherein die Lösung des kaum geschürzten Knotens in die Hand zu geben," Wellhausen, "Review of August Dillmann, *Hiob*," 555 (compare the discussion in Müller, *Das Hiobproblem*, 37). The closest parallel in the Hebrew Bible is Gen 22:1; compare B. Jacob, *Das erste Buch der Tora: Genesis* (Berlin: Schocken, 1934) 491–92; C. Westermann, *Genesis 12–36* (BK I/2; Neukirchen-Vluyn: Neukirchener Verlag, 1981), 436; Blum, *Vätergeschichte*, 329 with n.113 (bibliography); T. Veijola, "Das Opfer des Abraham—Paradigma des Glaubens aus dem nachexilischen Zeitalter," *ZTK* 85 (1988) 129–64 (here 139–40, 151); idem, "Abraham und Hiob: Das literarische Verhältnis von Gen 22 und der Hiob-Novelle," in *Vergegenwärtigung des Alten Testaments: Beiträge zur biblischen Hermeneutik* (ed. C. Bultmann et al.; Göttingen: Vandenhoeck & Ruprecht, 2002) 127–55; J. Ebach, "Theodizee: Fragen gegen die Antworten. Anmerkungen zur biblischen Erzählung von der 'Bindung Isaaks' (1 Mose 22)," in *Gott im Wort: Drei Studien zur biblischen Exegese und Hermeneutik* (Neukirchen-Vluyn: Neukirchener Verlag, 1997) 1–25; H. Strauß, "Zu Genesis 22 und dem erzählenden Rahmen des Hiobbuches (Hiob 1,1–2,10 und 42,7–17)," in *Verbindungslinien* (ed. A. Graupner et al.; Neukirchen-Vluyn: Neukirchener Verlag, 2000) 377–83; K. Schmid, "Die Rückgabe der Verheißungsgabe: Der 'heilsgeschichtliche' Sinn von Genesis 22 im Horizont innerbiblischer Exegese," pp. 271–300 in *Gott und Mensch im Dialog* (ed. M. Witte; BZAW 345/I; Berlin: de Gruyter, 2004) 271–300.

Wellhausen and many following him assume that the narrator made a conceptual mistake when incorporating older material, the "folk tale" mentioned earlier. He argues that, when determining the position of the author in regard to the issue of theodicy, one must disregard the prologue. Yet, the view that the proleptic solution to the Job problem (proleptic in regard to the book as a whole) was a merely unfortunate by-product of the compilation of different sources was unconvincing even in the context of classic literary-critical assumptions. It fails completely once we entertain the notion of a basic literary interconnection between the frame and the dialogues.

I believe that we can make a strong and much more plausible case for the opposite hypothesis: the combination of the proleptic solution to the Job problem in the prologue with the later solutions in the rest of the book stands as the center of the theology of the author of the book of Job.

The following considerations provide explanation for this statement: first of all, the readers are given a unique perspective from which to evaluate the friends' explanations for Job's suffering, which appear from chapter three on. The friends move through almost the entire spectrum of possible explanations for the Job problem. Perhaps Job refuses to admit he has sinned, or he has sinned unconsciously. Perhaps he has to suffer because he—like all other human beings—is guilty by nature und must be educated in a certain manner.[56] The friends argue back and forth within these possibilities. Job, however, rebels against all of these explanations, and the readers of the book know that he is right!

Job's suffering cannot be explained by anything Job has done against God, nor is it the result of the fact that humans cannot be justified in the eyes of God. Even the idea of divine pedagogy is not correct. The reason for Job's suffering lies solely in a cruel heavenly test, to which God and the *satan* have subjected Job. The prologue makes this absolutely clear.

What does this mean? The sequence of prologue and dialogues seems to be arranged in such a manner in order that the positions of the friends in the dialogues are criticized from the beginning. Whatever thoughts the friends entertain may be part of a usual repertoire of theological insights into the Job problem, but the prologue states in rebuttal: all this has nothing to do with what is actually happening. The logic of heaven is completely different than that used by the friends. It is so different that no one would even think of it unless they were given insight into heaven itself. In

---

56. On the distinction between these two concepts, see E. W. Nicholson, "The Limits of Theodicy as a Theme of the Book of Job," in *Wisdom in Ancient Israel* (ed. J. Day et al.; Cambridge: Cambridge University Press, 1995) 71–82.

the light of the prologue, the friends' theology is reduced to nothing more than speculation about God that has nothing to do with God himself.[57]

The prologue is not only relevant for the friends' speeches but also— and perhaps more importantly—for the divine monologues that follow the dialogues in Job 38:1–40:2 and 40:6–41:26. After the friends' explanations, God himself speaks to Job. God speaks at length and with gravity. If we survey the more recent literature on Job, we frequently encounter the statement that the divine monologues constitute the climax of the entire book.[58] God authoritatively solves the Job problem, and his monologues determine the intention of the book as a whole.

---

57. For a different view, see J. W. Watts, ("The Unreliable Narrator of Job," in *The Whirlwind: Essays on Job—Hermeneutics and Theology in Memory of Jane Morse* [ed. S. L. Cook, C. L. Patton, and J. W. Watts; JSOTSup 336; Sheffield: Sheffield Academic Press, 2001] 168–80), who draws the contrary conclusion that the divine speeches falsify the prologue. Scherer, *Lästiger Trost*, 12, has made a remarkable case in favor of the friends, especially Eliphaz: "Man wird kaum annehmen dürfen, dass nichts von dem, was die Freunde tatsächlich zu sagen haben, den Fall Hiob tatsächlich berührt." . . . "Sonst hätte der Dichter nicht so viele Kapitel damit angefüllt." The sheer volume of the friends' speeches is indeed noteworthy and in need of explanation. The reason for this may lie in the fact that everything the friends have to say is part of *traditional logic* on this matter and thus must take up this much space. As true as Scherer's objection against a general defamation of the friends is, one must still take the narrative shape of the book of Job seriously when interpreting this text.

58. See Duhm, *Buch Hiob*, IX: The divine monologues provide "die letzten Aufschlüsse und den letzten Trost erteilen"; G. von Rad, *Die Theologie der geschichtlichen Überlieferungen Israels* (Vol. 1 of *Theologie des Alten Testaments*; 10th ed.; Munich: Kaiser, 1992), 413: "Diese Gottesreden wird man nun doch bei aller gebotenen Scheu, die innere Komplexität des Werkes zu vereinfachen, als den Höhepunkt verstehen dürfen, der nach dem Verständnis des Dichters das Ringen Hiobs zu einem Abschluß bringt"; M. Tsevat, "The Meaning of the Book of Job," *HUCA* 37 (1966) 73–106 (here 82): "the Book of Job presents a problem (it is the problem of the suffering of the innocent); the problem has an answer; the answer is contained in the final chapters; and the final chapters are authentic"; Schmid, *Wesen und Geschichte der Weisheit*, 180; Crüsemann, "Hiob und Kohelet," 374–75: "Der Schlüssel zum Verständnis der Hiobdichtung liegt ganz ohne Zweifel in der Gottesrede Hi 38ff."; A. Brenner, "God's Answer to Job," *VT* 31 (1981) 129–37 (here 129): "Presumably, God's words should constitute the climax of the book as a whole, and elaborate the religious philosophy of the author who composed these chapters"; H. Gese, "Die Frage nach dem Lebenssinn: Hiob und die Folgen," *ZTK* 79 (1982) 161–79 (here 170): "Die Lösung des Hiobbuchs erfolgt in der Gottesvision mit den beiden Gottesreden"; H. Rowold, "Yahweh's Challenge to Rival: The Form and Function of the Yahweh-Speech in Job 38–39," *CBQ* 47 (1985) 199–211 (here 199): "That the Yahweh-Speeches form the literary and theological climax of the Book of Job is commonly recognized"; J. E. Miller, "Structure and Meaning of the Animal Discourse in the Theophany of Job (38,39–39,30)," *ZAW* 103 (1991) 418–21 (here 418): "The theophany of the Book of Job is vital for understanding the answer which the book offers to the problem of theodicy"; Crenshaw, "Job, Book of," 862: "Presumably, the author's answer . . . is hidden within the divine speeches"; Lévêque ("L'interprétation de discours," 203) refers to the divine speeches as "clef principale d'interprétation pour le livre de Job"; see also B. Lang, "Ijob (Buch)," *Neues Bibel-Lexikon* 7:215–18 (here 217–18); Kuhl (*TR* 1954, 303–14) lists further solutions to the Job-problem (see Fohrer, *Buch Hiob*, 557).

At first glance, this solution does not seem plausible. Even a surface reading of the divine monologues shows that they provide detailed information on the origin of hail, the labor pains of the doe, the leap of the locust, the nest of the eagle, thunder and lightning, the hippopotamus and the crocodile—but no word is said about Job and his suffering.

This is why many have understood these monologues quite differently and referred to them as "three hours of biology lessons for Job"[59] or as "magnificent irrelevance."[60]

Othmar Keel's[61] iconographic analysis, however, has shown that such ridicule falls short of the text; Keel demonstrated that the divine speeches are indeed linked closely to the Job problem. The description of the regular order of creation as well as the motives of chaos embodied in the hippopotamus and the crocodile refer to a creation order that may not mention Job's suffering directly, but they provide a larger context for understanding his suffering. Job may suffer, but Job is not the world. Job's life may be breaking down, but the world is functioning nicely. Job may be surrounded by chaos, but creation as a whole is a cosmos structured and maintained by God.

Following the friend's failed attempts to find a solution to the Job problem, attempts that Job rejects in total, the divine monologues authoritatively present *their* answer, which is eventually accepted by Job. This answer goes as follows: "There is order"[62] in the universe, even if this order remains hidden from Job. God is the wise creator of his world,

---

For a survey of scholarship on the divine monologues, see D. Gowan, "God's Answer to Job: How Is It an Answer," *HBT* 8 (1986) 85–102 (here 87–89).

59. L. Steiger, "Die Wirklichkeit Gottes in unserer Verkündigung," in *Auf dem Wege zu schriftgemäßer Verkündigung* (ed. M. Honecker and L. Steiger; BEvT 39; Munich: Kaiser, 1965) 143–77 (here 160).

60. C. J. Ball, *The Book of Job: A Revised Text and Version* (Oxford: Clarendon, 1922) 2. See also the critical evaluation of the divine monologues in E. Greenstein, "In Job's Face/ Facing Job," in *The Labour of Reading: Desire, Alienation, and Biblical Interpretation* (ed. F. C. Black et al.; Atlanta: SBL 1999) 301–17; A. LaCocque, "The Deconstruction of Job's Fundamentalism," *JBL* 126 (2007) 83–97 (but compare P. Guillaume, "Dismantling the Deconstruction of Job." *JBL* 127 [2008] 491–99).

61. *Jahwes Entgegnung an Ijob*; see also M. Oeming, "Kannst du der Löwin ihren Raub zu jagen geben?" (Hi 38,39): Das Motiv des "Herrn der Tiere" und seine Bedeutung für die Theologie der Gottesreden Hi 38–42," in *"Dort ziehen Schiffe dahin": Collected Communications to the XIVth Congress of the International Organization for the Study of the Old Testament: Paris 1992* (ed. M. Augustin and K. D. Schunck; BEAT 28; Frankfurt a.M.: Lang, 1992) 147–63; K. Baltzer and T. Krüger, "Die Erfahrung Hiobs: 'Konnektive' und 'distributive' Gerechtigkeit nach dem Hiob-Buch," in *Problems in Biblical Theology.* (ed. H. T. C. Sun et al. Grand Rapids: Eerdmans, 1997) 27–37 (here 35); a similar comment is already found in M. Buber, *Der Glaube der Propheten* (Zurich: Manesse, 1950) 278.

62. Schmid, *Wesen und Geschichte der Weisheit*, 181.

which he cultivates and guides, even where this cannot be recognized by human beings.[63]

Nonetheless, the prologue creates quite a different frame for interpreting the divine monologues. The prologue presents a different view of God's ordered creation: Job's suffering is *not* part of God's created order, not even part of an invisible and dynamic order. It is the result of an unusually cruel test that heaven performs on Job—a test that is never actually made clear: God does not even hint at the events that transpired in heaven when answering Job.[64] God speaks to Job, but he does not tell him what is actually going on.

The readers, however, are informed by the prologue and thus hear the divine speeches with different ears: The created order described in Job 38–41 presents itself not simply as proof of God's rule over a dynamic world, it mutates to an *alibi*, a cover-up of the true reason for Job's suffering. Whatever the case may be—be it that God does not think that Job could handle the reason or does not want to burden him with it—God withholds the answer from Job. The fact that the *satan* incited God is none of Job's business, even though its consequences had an existential impact on his life, even destroyed him.[65]

---

63. See Newsom, *Book of Job*, 252: "From the striking metaphor of the sea as a swaddled infant, to the celebration of the wildness of those creatures who mock and spurn human control, to the ecstatic description of Leviathan, the uncomfortable sense grows that God's identification with the chaotic is as strong as with symbols of order." See also eadem, "Re-considering Job," 170. Newsom goes on to point out the emphasis on spatial distance between the realms of God's creative activity and Job: "the foundations of the earth, the doors of the primordial sea, the horizon of dawn, the recesses of the sea and the gates of death, the home from which night and darkness emerge, the storage places of snow, hail, rain, and wind. . . . [T]he contrast between the way space is imagined could not be more radical" (*Book of Job*, 240; similar in LaCocque, "The Deconstruction of Job's Fundamentalism," 2007, 86–87).

64. This remarkable feature is strikingly seldom mentioned in secondary literature: see J. Joosten ("La macrostructure du livre de Job et quelques parallèles (Jérémie 45; 1 Rois 19)," *The Book of Job* [ed. W. A. M.Beuken; BETL 114; Leuven: Peeters, 1994] 400–404 [here 400], with reference to M. Greenberg, "Reflections on Job's Theology," in *Studies in Bible and Jewish Thought* [Philadelphia: Jewish Publication Society, 1995] 327–333); see, however, C. R. Seitz, "Job: Full-Structure, Movement and Interpretation," *Interpretation* 43 (1989) 5–17 (here 14–15); A. E. Steinmann, "The Structure and Message of the Book of Job," *VT* 46 (1996) 85–100; T. Krüger, "Einheit und Vielfalt des Göttlichen nach dem Alten Testament," in *Trinität* (ed. W. Härle and R. Preul; Marburger Jahrbuch Theologie X; Marburger theologische Studien 49; Marburg: Elwert, 1998) 16–50 (here, 24): "Dabei überrascht es vor allem, daß Gott selbst, der Hiob in Kap. 38–41 ausführlich über sein Handeln in der Welt belehrt, mit keinem Wort auf die Vorgänge im himmlischen Hofstaat eingeht, von denen Kap. 1–2 erzählte."

65. It should be noted that God never speaks of himself as "Yhwh" but as "El," "Eloah," or "Šaddai" (see A. LaCocque, "Job or the Impotence of Religion and Philosophy," *Semeia* 19 [1981] 33–52).

The divine speeches thus become strangely ambivalent from the read-ers' point of view: the conglomeration of rhetorical questions posed by God impressively presents his sovereign rule, but a bitter taste remains. Can God's sovereignty not afford to let Job know the true reason for his suffering? In the light of the prologue, the divine speeches lose much of their luster. The prologue divides divine revelation and truth and drives a wedge between them.

Thus, the same theme is continued that was already observed in regard to the dialogues: the prologue not only criticizes the friends' theology; it also criticizes God's revelation. From the perspective of the prologue, God can be understood on the basis neither of human nor of divine speech.

How then can we speak of God at all? Only in the manner of the prologue? Only here do we find clear information on what is happening between God and Job. The text states clearly why Job has to suffer: Job is the victim of a test. Yet we rightly hesitate before accepting the prologue as the final authority on the secrets of heaven. The reason for this hesita-tion lies in the fairy-tale-like character of the prologue mentioned earlier.[66] In regard to the scenes in heaven, the fairy-tale quality is produced by the unreal narrative perspective of the description.[67] It is important to note in this context that the text does not convey any information on how this revelation was made possible: There is no mention of an opening of the heavens, no prophetic seer appears who may possess insight into heaven; instead, the text simply reports what is supposed to have happened there.

The fairy-tale quality is also produced by the literary shape of the pro-logue. At the beginning of the book, Job is introduced as "blameless and upright"; he "fears God and avoids evil" (Job 1:1). This very description reappears in God's mouth in 1:8 when he says to the *satan*: "Have you paid attention to my servant Job? There is none like him on earth: He is blameless and upright, fears God, and avoids evil." The narrative spheres of heaven and earth and the characters therein are thus fully aligned, pro-ducing a strangely artificial atmosphere.

The description of events on earth also show the same artificiality, which clearly refers to the fictional nature of the narrative: Job must be the *greatest* of all the sons of the east (Job 1:3), there is *none* like him on

---

66. On "fairy tales" in the Hebrew Bible, see F. Ahuis, "Das Märchen im Alten Testa-ment." *ZTK* 86 (1989) 455–76; H.-J. Hermisson, "Märchen II," *TRE* 21: 672–77.

67. On this, see J. C. de Moor on Ugarit ("The Crisis of Polytheism in Late Bronze Ugarit," in *Crises and Perspectives: Studies in Ancient Near Eastern Polytheism, Biblical Theo-logy, Palestinian Archaeology and Intertestamental Literature* [ed. J. C. de Moor; OTS 24; Leiden: Brill, 1986] 1–20), for an analysis within the context of comparative religious history.

earth (1:8),[68] he must lose *all* of his possessions and *all* of his children on *one* day (1:13ff.).[69] The commentary on Job by Franz Hesse exclaims in disbelief: "Such massive catastrophe simply does not happen in real life!"[70] In contrast to Hesse, however, we are not dealing with a case of hyperbole gone wrong but with intentional narrative shape. The prologue of the book of Job presents us with intentionally fractured fiction.

The proverbial bad news presented to Job in 1:13–19 is written with stereotypical phrases. In reversed sequence, Job loses everything he owned as recorded in 1:2–3.[71] This stereotypical language is not without its own artistry, noted as early as Wellhausen, who commented: "Any variation would be a loss."[72] The four messengers successively interrupt each other and 1:16, 17, and 18 each state with precisely the same words: "As this one was still speaking, another came and said. . . ." This stereotypical language is heightened by the identical closing phrases of each catastrophic message. None of the messengers is aware of the speech of his predecessor, yet each closes with the statement: "I, I alone escaped in order to tell you."[73]

These literary observations can be supplemented by a further thematic oddity—that is, the burnt offerings (עלות) that Job performs every morning following a celebration put on by his children. "Perhaps"—as it is explicitly stated in Job 1:5—"they may have sinned." Job attempts to insure himself against this "perhaps" by proactively performing an offering

---

68. Classic Jewish exegesis already noted that Job is placed much higher than Abraham or Moses due to this characterization (see Hoffman, "The Relation between the Prologue and the Speech-Cycles in Job," 165 and the reference in n. 11). The Talmud contains the statement that Job never existed but was only a parable (משל) (see Joosten, "La macrostructure du livre de Job," 400). See also W. Vogels, "Job's Empty Pious Slogans (Job 1,20–22; 2,8–10)," in *The Book of Job* (ed. W. A. M.Beuken; BETL 114; Leuven: Peeters, 1994) 369–76.

69. See D. J. A. Clines, "False Naivety in the Prologue to Job," *HAR* 9 (1985) 127–36 (here 127); see also Brenner, "God's Answer to Job," 40: "Job is set before the reader as an impossible example!"; Hoffman, "The Relation between the Prologue and the Speech-Cycles in Job," 165: "a sterilized, utopian, superhuman personage like Job."

70. F. Hesse, *Hiob* (ZBK 14; Zurich: TVZ, 1978) 31 ["So massiv katastrophal geht es im wirklichen Leben nun doch nicht zu!"].

71. See the tables in S. Meier, "Job I–III: A Reflection of Genesis I–III, *VT* 39 (1989) 183–93 (here 188). On the inner order of the catastrophes, see Clines, *Job 1–20*, 30; for a sociological analysis, see R. Albertz, "Der sozialgeschichtliche Hintergrund des Hiobbuchs und der 'Babylonischen Theodizee'," in *Die Botschaft und die Boten* (ed. J. Jeremias and L. Perlitt; Neukirchen-Vluyn: Neukirchener Verlag, 1981) 107–34; repr. in *Geschichte und Theologie: Studien zur Exegese des Alten Testaments und zur Religionsgeschichte Israels* (BZAW 326; Berlin: de Gruyter, 2003) 349–72; Crüsemann, "Hiob und Kohelet," 386–93.

72. Wellhausen, "Review of August Dillmann, *Hiob*," 555 ("Es wäre schade um jede Abwechslung").

73. See the thoughts in Ebach, *Streiten mit Gott*, 20–25.

before he can even know whether or not his children actually did something wrong.

Even if the Hebrew Bible elsewhere describes atonement offerings to deal with unconscious sins (שגגה; see especially Lev 5:1–13[74]), Job's offering remains unique, because it is substitutionary and occurs in advance of any acknowledgment of sin.

We cannot explain this fact by stating that other biblical characters were simply less pious than Job; the oddity stems from the fact that such an "offering as insurance" is theologically absurd.[75] A burnt offering such as those performed by Job is an atonement offering, designed to atone for sin not to insure possible human misdeeds against divine retribution. The fact that neither the narrator nor God criticize this action is no argument against the absurdity of this offering; instead, this silence readily fits into the specific narrative shape of the prologue.

In spite of the drama of all that happens, and in spite of the harshness of the blows that befall Job, we recognize clearly: Job is a paradigm, not

74. See R. Rendtorff, *Studien zur Geschichte des Opfers im Alten Israel* (WMANT 24; Neukirchen-Vluyn: Neukirchener Verlag, 1967) 200–205; idem, *Leviticus* (BK III Fasc. 2/3; Neukirchen-Vluyn: Neukirchener Verlag, 1990/1992) at this verse; H. Gese, "Die Sühne," in *Zur biblischen Theologie: Alttestamentliche Vorträge* (BEvT 78; Munich: Kaiser, 1977) 85–106 (here 101); B. Janowski, *Sühne als Heilsgeschehen: Studien zur Sühmetheologie der Priesterschrift und zur Wurzel* KPR *im Alten Orient und im Alten Testament* (WMANT 55; Neukirchen-Vluyn: Neukirchener Verlag, 1982) 254–59; F. Crüsemann, *Die Tora: Theologie und Sozialgeschichte des alttestamentlichen Gesetzes* (Munich: Kaiser, 1992) 370–74; H. Utzschneider, "Vergebung im Ritual: Zur Deutung des חטאת-Rituals im Sündopfer," in *Abschied von der Schuld? Zur Anthropologie und Theologie von Schuldbekenntnis, Opfer und Versöhnung* (ed. R. Riess; Stuttgart: Kohlhammer, 1996) 96–119; see also the contributions by D. Daube, *Sin, Ignorance and Forgiveness in the Bible* (London: Liberal Jewish Synagogue 1960); A. Schenker, "Der Unterschied zwischen Sündopfer חטאת und Schuldopfer אשם im Licht von Lev 5,17–19 und 5,1–6," in *Recht und Kult im Alten Testament: Achtzehn Studien* (ed. A. Schenker; OBO 172; Fribourg: Universitätsverlag/Göttingen: Vandenhoeck & Ruprecht, 2000) 104–12; idem, "Keine Versöhnung ohne Anerkennung der Haftung für verursachten Schaden: Die Rolle von Haftung und Intentionalität in den Opfern חטאת und אשם (Lev 4–5)," in *Recht und Kult im Alten Testament: Achtzehn Studien* (ed. A. Schenker; OBO 172; Fribourg: Universitätsverlag/Göttingen: Vandenhoeck & Ruprecht, 2000) 113–22.

75. See A. Brenner, "Job the Pious? The Characterization of Job in the Narrative Framework of the Book," *JSOT* 43 (1989) 37–52 (here 44): "The religiosity of Job is almost a parody of faith rather than a climactic manifestation of it"; see also Clines, *Job 1–20*, 15: "Job's piety is scrupulous, even excessively so, if not actually neurotically anxious" (cf. bibliography). This also applies to the proposal by Müller ("Die Hiobrahmenerzählung und ihre alt-orientalischen Parallelen," 24 n. 18), who assumes based on wisdom literature's lacking interest in cultic matters that Job's interest in offerings is due to the "folk-tale" character of the prose frame. See also M. Oeming, "Il offrait un holocauste pour chacun d'eux" (Job 1,5): Pourquoi pas pour lui-même? Opfer und Nicht-Opfer im Hiobbuch, *RHPR* 93 (2013) 49–65.

a person. Job is not a historical case-study; Job is the character in a novel that does not report experience but condenses it. To say it with a phrase from Elie Wiesel:[76] Job never lived, but he suffered greatly.[77]

How are we to understand the fractured narrative of the prologue? The following idea emerges: just as the prologue forms a counterweight against the dialogues and the divine speeches, it also contains a critical counterweight against itself. The prologue thus embodies the unity of criticism and self-criticism.

The prologue of the book of Job is shaped like a fairy tale in order to prevent us from using it as the Archimedean point from which to set the book in motion and speculate on God and the world. The fairy-tale quality is not merely there as a container of content, but the form itself signals theological criticism of what is presented: the unreal perspective embodied in the prologue remains fictional and the prologue is very aware of this.

What do these thoughts imply for the theology of the book Job? We gain the impression that the book of Job, read from the perspective of the prologue, embodies all the characteristics of negative theology. All affirmative speech about God is called into question by the prologue. The prologue suspends the logic of the friends' theology in the dialogues, it suspends the finality of the divine speeches, and it even suspends its own logic to a certain degree. The prologue thus successively lays out all possible solutions to the reason for Job's suffering: theological speculation as contained in the dialogues, divine revelation as contained in the monologues of God, even metaphysical constructions as presented in the prologue. All these options must be discarded as solutions to the Job problem.

By using a sophisticated system of literary *checks and balances* between the prologue, the dialogues and the divine speeches, the book of Job does not answer the problem that stands at its center. Instead, by criticizing each of its own answers, it thrusts the problem back at its readers.[78] This process of giving back the problem is a process of theological education that is designed to reject any objectified speech about God, which turns God into an object of reflection or projection. Who or what God may be is outside of human grasp—this is the message of the book of Job.

---

76. E. Wiesel, *Adam oder das Geheimnis des Anfangs* (2nd ed.; Freiburg: Herder, 1982) 211 (see Ebach, *Streiten mit Gott*, IX). Against T. N. D. Mettinger ("The Enigma of Job: The Deconstruction of God in Intertextual Perspective," *JNSWL* 23 [1997] 1–19 [here 3]), it is not plausible to assume that the author's own experiences stand behind Job.

77. For a survey of scholarship on the historicity of Job, see H. H. Rowley, "The Book of Job and Its Meaning," 172 n. 3–4.

78. See Köhlmoos, *Das Auge Gottes*.

Within the context of the Hebrew Bible, the book of Job thus primarily contradicts the God of justice as presented by the prophets:[79] God, as Job shows us, can destroy us without reason. It also contradicts the merciful God of Priestly literature:[80] we must accept God not only as the present God; he is also the absent God. Finally, the book of Job also provides, in some of its parts, a parody on the piety of the Psalms: Job's situation transcends the options for reaching God provided by the Psalms.[81]

For the book of Job, God is not just or merciful, yet he is also not unjust or cruel; instead God is—God.[82] In the context of these various biblical positions, this statement is more than mere tautology, it is a critical position all its own. It is a striking statement, because it shows us that speaking of God was no easier in antiquity, with its mythically charged worldview, than it is for modern times.

5. Conclusion

With this position, the book of Job as a whole coincides to a remarkable degree with the basic melody of the divine speeches. There is no way to claim justice against God's injustice as experienced by Job. God is not subjected to any overarching principles; he remains fully sovereign. In this regard, but only in this regard, classic scholarship on the book of Job proves correct when it states that the divine monologues are the thematic center of the entire book.

The critical retraction of all affirmative speech about God in the book of Job may sound resigned, it may sound agnostic, it may even sound like the end of all theology. But we have to be careful. The book of Job does not promote silence about God because we cannot say anything about him. Otherwise, this book would never have been written. But the book of Job does bid farewell to certain types of theology—and we do not have to bemoan their loss: theology as the wisdom of the world projected into heaven; theology as pious reflection on a higher being that then mistakes

---

79. See Whybray, "The Immorality of God," 110; the material in H. Bardtke, ("Prophetische Züge im Buche Hiob," in *Das ferne und das nahe Wort* [ed. Fritz Maass; BZAW 105; Berlin: de Gruyter, 1967] 1–10) should be evaluated in this context.

80. See especially Knauf, "Hiobs Heimat," 82; similar material in M. Fishbane, "Jeremiah IV 23–26 and Job III 3–13: A Recovered Use of the Creation Pattern;" *VT* 21 (1971) 151–67.

81. See W. Kynes, *My Psalm Has Turned into Weeping: Job's Dialogue with the Psalms* (BZAW 437; Berlin: de Gruyter, 2012); see also K. Dell and W. Kynes, *Reading Job Intertextually* (LHB/OTS 574; London: Continuum, 2012).

82. See the statement in Tsevat, "The Meaning of the Book of Job," 105: "He Who speaks to man in the Book of Job is neither a just nor an injust god but God."

traditional or innovative ideas about God *entirely* for God himself; theology that purports to communicate direct revelation from God. The book of Job distrusts and disbelieves all this to its core. Instead, it states clearly that this is not God; these are only graven images. Such fundamental criticism of all pseudo-theology is—and here we can only agree with the book of Job—not the end but the very beginning of theology.[83]

We might criticize the book of Job for saying too little about God. We could ask whether sovereignty can exist outside of the paths of power and its indiscriminate use, or we could ask whether it is feasible to play the divinity of God against God's mercy and justice.

We should, however, give the book of Job credit for three things. (1) The book of Job is wisdom literature, and a good rule of thumb for wisdom literature is to say rather too little than too much. (2) There is definitely also a time for theological restraint. (3) The book of Job is very aware of the fact that its extreme celebration of God's sovereignty does not exclude but rather includes God's justice and grace. This is what the ending of the book tells us—an ending that hypercritical individuals have always tried to portray as being superfluous. Here, Job's fortune is restored. At the same time, this also remains true of the just and merciful God: he is no *servant* of his justice and grace.

---

83. The book of Job itself points toward an idea of what proper speech of God may look like. This idea results from the concept of the book as a whole in connection with the key verse in Job 42:7: "My wrath has been kindled against you and your friends, for you have not spoke correctly to me (כי לא דברתם עלי) as my servant Job has. M. Oeming ("'Ihr habt nicht recht von mir geredet wie mein Knecht Hiob'—Gottes Schlusswort als Schlüssel zur Interpretation des Hiobbuchs und als kritische Anfrage an die moderne Theologie," *EvT* 60 [2000] 103–16; repr. in *Hiobs Weg* [ed. idem and K. Schmid; Neukirchen-Vluyn: Neukirchener Verlag, 2001] 125–47; see also chapter 6 below) has convincingly shown—in conceptual and semantic connection to the book as a whole—that דבר על should be understood as "speaking to" and not "speaking of." As much as the idea of *disputare de deo* is rejected, the book of Job continues to advocate a form of speech transformed through suffering: lament as speech to God. Instead of speculation about God, the book advocates existential and authentic speech to God. See also H. G. Reventlow, "Skepsis und Klage: Zur Komposition des Hiobbuches," in *Verbindungslinien* (ed. A. Graupner et al.; Neukirchen-Vluyn: Neukirchener Verlag, 2000) 281–94; G. Wallis, "Das Hiobbuch – Komplexität und Kontingenz," in *Verbindungslinien* (ed. A. Graupner et al.; Neukirchen-Vluyn: Neukirchener Verlag, 2000) 413–26 (here 425); K. Engljähringer, *Theologie im Streitgespräch*, 195; I. Kottsieper, "'Thema verfehlt!' Zur Kritik Gottes an den drei Freunden in Hi 42,7–9," in *Gott und Mensch im Dialog* (ed. M. Witte; BZAW 345/II; Berlin: de Gruyter, 2004) 777–85 (here 780), presents a different interpretation of Job 42:7: "Das Hiobbuch bietet nun mit seinen vier Belegen für die Langform אלי an Stelle von אל (3,22; 5,26; 15,22; 29,19) die Möglichkeit אלנכון על ohne eine Änderung des Konsonantentextes im Sinne von 'hinsichtlich dessen, was dasteht', d.h. 'hinsichtlich dessen, was Sache ist' zu verstehen." Kottsieper's interpretation is, however, based on a certain thematic criticism of Oeming's interpretation (777–78), which does not necessarily lead to a different reading of Job 42:7.

CHAPTER 2

The Dialogues with Job's Wife and Friends

MANFRED OEMING

There are good reasons to read the dialogues between Job, his wife, his friends, God, and finally his internal dialogue as case studies in pastoral theology (poimenics).[1] I would define poimenics as *the art of leading an individual suffering in body or spirit to true self-knowledge by making him aware of God's being and actions. This self-awareness includes correction of false attitudes and provides comfort and support.* The book of Job certainly occupies an elevated position among all biblical contributions to poimenics.[2] This position is due to the multiplicity of different stereotypi-

---

1. See T. Mickel, *Seelsorgerliche Aspekte im Hiobbuch: Ein Beitrag zur biblischen Dimension der Poimenik* (Theologische Arbeiten 48; Berlin: Evangelische Verlagsanstalt, 1990). R. Albertz, *Vom Exil bis zu den Makkabäern*, vol. 2 of *Religionsgeschichte Israels in Alttestamentlicher Zeit* (ATD Ergänzung 8/2; Göttingen: Vandenhoeck & Ruprecht, 1992) 561–69, also places this aspect at the center of his interpretation.

2. B. Amrein, "Auch wenn die Finsternis noch wächst: Erfahrungen einer Krankenhaus-Seelsorgerin," *BK* 47 (1992) 123–24; U. Bach, "Mit behinderten Menschen das Evangelium neu entdecken: Seelsorgliche Erfahrungen und theologische Anfragen," *BTZ* 11 (1994) 107–23; G. Barth, "Schutz des Lebens und Liebesgebot: Theologische Erwägungen für Seelsorger und Berater," in *Neutestamentliche Versuche und Beobachtungen* (ed. G. Barth; Wechselwirkungen 4; Waltrop: H. Spinner, 1996) 283–97; I. Baumgartner, "Von Gott Geschichten erzählen: Pastoralpsychologische Anregungen für eine narrative Seelsorge," *BL* 67 (1994) 203–209; R. Gebauer, *Paulus als Seelsorger: Ein exegetischer Beitrag zur praktischen Theologie* (Calwer theologisches Monographien A/18; Stuttgart: Calwer 1997); W. Grimm, *Fürchte dich nicht Ein exegetischer Zugang zum Seelsorgepotential einer deuterojesajanischen Gattung* (Europäische Hochschulschriften 23/ 298; Frankfurt: Lang, 1986); A. Rinn-Maurer, *Seelsorge an Herzpatienten: Zum interdisziplinären Gespräch zwischen Medizin und Theologie* (AzTh 81; Stuttgart: Calwer, 1995); H.-J. Stoebe, "Jeremia, Prophet und Seelsorger," in *Geschichte, Schicksal, Schuld und Glaube* (Edited by H.-J. Stoebe; BBB 72; Frankfurt a.M.: Athenäum, 1989) 184–208; A. Tafferner, "Was trauen wir der Bibel in der Seelsorge zu?" *BL* 69 (1996) 255–57; E. Vellmer, "Verantwortlich reden von Gott am Krankenbett," in *Rudolf Bultmanns Werk und Wirkung* (ed. B. Jaspert; Darmstadt: Wissenschaftliche Buchgesellschaft, 1984) 426–42; H. Werners, "Der Seelsorger in der

cal characters that each articulate their own reaction to the suffering of Job and thus provide us with *a brief typology of possible strategies of pastoral care*. It is plausible to read the book as a classical case study for counseling. The following chapter aims to uncover various counseling "strategies" and evaluate them in the light of contemporary studies on counseling.[3]

1. Job's Self-counseling

1. The biblical Job in chapters 1 and 2 displays remarkable *self-control*. His equanimity seems to be an important facet—even proof—of his fear of God. He shows us that the thoughts of—perhaps especially of—the suffering individual are not free; he is called to accept the sovereignty of God and remain silent. "In all this he did not sin with his lips" (Job 2:10; compare 1:20). This statement implies a certain ideal: patient and silent acceptance of suffering that bears all with stoic fortitude, no matter what happens.

Perhaps this human virtue mirrors a certain view of God, which we encounter, for example, in the divine speech in Isa 45:7:

> I form the light and create darkness, I bring prosperity and create disaster; I, the LORD, do all these things.

If the almighty causes *everything*, then human beings encounter God in the totality of their experience—they encounter a God who is always justified, no matter what he does. This type of theology requires utter humility on the part of human beings. Whatever rage may boil inside of Job, in deference to God he is called to remain silent. We can read the book of Job as a journey that starts in complete submission and then erupts into wild rebellion and endless demand for justice before returning back to devotion (Job 42:1–6). Job's theologically motivated *self-control* stands at the

---

Spannung zwischen biblischer Weisung und Erfahrung der betroffenen Gläubigen," in *Geschieden–Wiederverheiratet–Abgewiesen? Antworten der Theologie* (ed. T. Schneider; QD 157 = Schriften der Europäischen Gesellschaft für Katholische Theologie 2; Freiburg: Herder 1995) 20–27; H. W. Wolff, "Humor als Seelsorge," in *Studien zur Prophetie: Probleme und Erträge* (ed. H. W. Wolff; TB 76; Munich: Kaiser, 1987) 124–28; J. Ziemer, "Schreie aus der Not, 1. Überlegungen für eine Seelsorge mit den Psalmen," in *Gottes Ehre erzählen* (ed. H. Seidel et al.; Leipzig: Thomas, 1994) 225–35.

3. It was an exemplary idea, because of its appropriateness, that C. Möller organized the volumes edited by him of *Geschichte der Seelsorge in Einzelportraits* (Vols. 1–4, Göttingen/Zurich 1994) to begin with contributions to counseling in the Bible. As a result, the potential for counseling contained in the Holy Scriptures is accorded appropriate appreciation and the discipline of poimeics is set on a proper foundation. In second position (after the Psalms) in the volume appears a relevant analysis of the book of Job by V. Weymann, "Hiob," in *Von Hiob bis Thomas von Kempen* (Vol. 1: 35–53).

beginning and the end of his journey.[4] Counseling, in this context, would imply the admonition to maintain one's self-control.

2. The biblical Job is not able to maintain his ataraxia for long. He is overwhelmed by the need to pour out his heart, *speak of the darkness of his soul, and cry his pain out to the world* (see 3:24).[5] The suffering individual is not able to keep his pain inside forever; he must communicate what he feels and talk about his thoughts and ideas, he must spit it out and thus

---

4. See similar advice in wisdom literature: cf. the analogous advice from the wisdom tradition, i.e.: "Discretion will protect you, and understanding will guard you" (Prov 2:11–12); a New Testament analogy is found in 2 Tim 1:7: "For God did not give us a spirit of timidity, but a spirit of power, of love and of self-discipline."

5. A wonderful description of the spirituality of lament is found in a sermon on Ps 88 by G. M. Martin (*Psalmenpredigten*, Stuttgart: Klotz), 1975, 23–31), a poem that is closely related to Job 3. Martin clearly describes the importance of crying out to God:

No comfort, no change, no miracle, no 'you, however . . .' no 'nevertheless'—only the harshness of reality, the harshness of the pain, which isolates, which delivers over to the present moment, a present without memory or hope. . . . And with all this he asserts, . . . that it is God, God himself who is silent, god who sleeps, God who hides his face, God who [simply] looks on, God who is like a foreigner, God who violates, God who chastens, God who disappoints bitterly, God who is distant. . . . I believe that we must reflect, along the lines of the lament psalms, on God, but also on the person as the one crying out because it is in no way self-explanatory that a person would lament and cry out at all—neither before God nor before another authority. . . . Desperate pain in the psalm is protest, outcry, opposition, irony, provocation. The lament is the last sign of a way out, the first step of liberation from voicelessness and powerlessness. If we take the psalm seriously, then we need not to learn comfort as much as to learn lament. We must not, by hook or by crook, interpret meaning into the meaninglessness, but rather to cry out the pain and meaninglessness. We should not use whatever means possible to quiet the one crying out; caressing them as long as it takes until they only whimper quietly and then say nothing more, can no longer lament. Instead, we should encourage them to cry out, listen to them, perhaps even cry out with them. The meaning of reality that expresses itself in this, which one attempts to change, to make better what is to be changed—this is one thing. The cry of the lament, the appraisal [of the situation] is something else, and this is primary. Theology is an endless study because it does not cope with or finish with its questions and answers. This is its strength and its weakness. For to understand the pain, it cannot suppress it. And every new suffering cries out for new comforters and theologians. And they come, but good and bad. The cry is the beginning of all theology. . . . The meaning of the cry became clearer for me than ever before this summer as I was part of a group on the California coast that practiced a kind of scream therapy. I experienced how years of muscle tension was relieved by screaming, how emotions that had been held back then erupted, how suddenly [internal] blockages ceased, how people screamed themselves hoarse because they had not screamed for twenty years. I experienced in myself and in others how we underwent and worked through old suppressed hurts and new present hurts, how all that causes us pain—screaming injustice, ignorance, foolishness, communication breakdown—how all of this causes us to suffer and to cry out. And the others and I experienced the power that is latent in screaming. Crying out is the first verbal form of resistance, a sign of the strength of protest, a sign that makes new life possible.

work through his pain. Following a period of silence, Job becomes talkative; his loathing of his existence breaks out. In a state of deep depression, he desires his own death (Job 3). After this eruption, he continues to describe his inner state of being in repeated, new attempts to communicate his plight. Interpreters of the book of Job have often complained that the dialogues in the middle section of the book show no continual train of thought, no progress of argument; this may be the case. Yet, from the perspective of counseling experience, we can recognize how wisely the poet turned these recurring waves of dark meditation into a text. The work of mourning does not consist of cognitive reflection structured in systematic progression leading to a simple conclusion. The same tiresome thoughts are entertained over and over again.

3. It seems that Job's most important form of self-comfort lies in his *never-ending affirmation of his own innocence*. It is almost a type of autosuggestion when Job assures the friends, God, and especially himself that he did not deserve this punishment (with special intensity in Job 9 and 31). The subjective conviction of his own blamelessness, which he postulates against the "dogma" of a causal connection between action and consequence, is a strong source of comfort. A necessary part of this comfort is the accusation against God:

> You, God, are to blame, not me. You have done injustice! I never did anything that may have contributed to this suffering; I never deserved this. The most merciless reflection of my conscience did not reveal any such sin. Just let me die and find peace in death!

4. The soul's most valuable path of communicating conflict with God is *lament*.[6] Lament is the courageous and uncompromisingly honest articulation of one's own feeling against all theological convention. In a kind of "lament against ones enemies," Job attacks his friends who not only appear to misunderstand him, but do not even seem to listen to him.

> Listen carefully to my words, and let this be your consolation. (Job 21:2)

Even if common theological interpretation of the world may abhor the idea of speaking so harshly to God, with increasing vehemence (provoked in part by the arguments of the friends), these accusations are the lifeblood of Job's continued existence. His accusation is a deep form of *prayer*; not

---

6. K. Seybold, "Psalmen im Buch Hiob," in *Studien zur Psalmenauslegung* (ed. K. Seybold; Stuttgart: Kohlhammer, 1998) 270–87; G. Steins, ed., *Schweigen wäre gotteslästerlich: Die heilende Kraft der Klage* (Würzburg: Echter, 2000).

a general reflection on the world, but communication with God. The frequent passages in which Job addresses God as "you" (see 7:12–21; 9:28–32; 10:2–18; 13:22–27; 14:13–20) are of high theological importance. This is exactly what Job is praised for in the end. Human beings can and should voice their lament to God.

5. In contrast to the friends, Job's speeches seem to indicate a hope that reaches beyond the limits of physical life. The passage in question is unclear and a matter of intense exegetical debate, yet I believe that the text in its final form (dated, most likely, to the Hellenistic period) shows that, in his despair, Job looks forward to a life to come.

> For I know that my Redeemer lives, and that at the last[7] he will stand upon the earth; and after my skin has been thus destroyed, then in my flesh I shall see God.[8]

---

7. It is remarkable that the preposition אחרון occurs frequently in the context of final revelations: see M. Oeming, "Gottes Offenbarung „von hinten," in *Gottes Offenbarung in der Welt* (ed. F. Krüger; Gütersloh: Gütersloher, 1998) 292–304. אחרון refers in this context to "far away days," future "Zukunft" (Isa 30:8) or "descendants" (Ps 48:14; 78:4, 6; 102:19; Prov 31:25). In Isa 44:6 and 48:12 it is even a kind of description of God: "I am *ʾaḥarōn*," usually translated as "the last" in contrast to "the first."

8. A. de Wilde, *Das Buch Hiob* (OTS 22; Leiden: Brill 1981) 214–15 summarizes the discussion well:

> The crux of the difference of opinion concerning the meaning of this verse is whether Job expects his justification or his death. If one assumes the latter, then there is space for the following views: (a) Job expects his resurrection from the dead in order to then be rehabilitated; this is the opinion of Clement of Rome, Origen, Augustine, and Jerome. The last of these translates, "I know that my redeemer lives, and that on the last day I will be resurrected from the earth and will be clothed with my skin, and in my body I will see my God." The later western translations (Luther, AV, StV, among others) are strongly influenced by this and offer similar renderings of this verse; (b) Job expects that after his death he will be justified in the realm of the dead (Ewald, Dillmann, Weiser, N. H. Ridderbos, Kroeze); (c) Job expects that God will lay out his justification before human witnesses after his death (Hölscher, Steeder); (d) Job expects that as a spirit he will see God himself; this will then be given as a sign, perhaps on his grave, in order to declare Job righteous (Duhm). We counter that none of these is possible. (a) The belief in resurrection is first evident in Israel in the second century B.C.; cf. Dan 1:22; 2 Macc 7:14; Wis 1:15, 3:5, 23; Isa 26:19. (b) Here a depiction of Sheol is assumed that does not agree with other statements about the nature of the realm of the dead in Job. (c) This would not be of any profit for Job in the realm of the dead; cf. 14:21. (d) Job's conviction is that, once one descends to the realm of the dead, there is no return; cf. 9:9–10, 10:21, 14:12, 18ff., 16:2, 17:13.

> [Der Kern der Meinungsverschiedenheit über die Bedeutung dieser Verse ist, ob Hiob seine Rechtfertigung vor oder nach dem Tode erwartet. Nimmt man das letztere an, dann gibt es Raum für die folgenden Auffassungen: a) Hiob erwartet seine Auferstehung von den Toten, um anschliessend rehabilitiert zu werden; so Clemens Romanus, Origenes, Augustinus, Hieronymus. Der Letztgenannte übersetzt: "Ich weiss, dass mein Erlöser lebt, und dass ich am jüngsten Tage aus der Erde auferstehen werde, und wieder bekleidet werde mit meiner Haut, und in

This comfort is expressed with the same reticence as in Ps 49:16,[9] yet it conveys a vague sense of eternity.

2. Job's Wife

The image of Job's wife as a counselor could hardly be worse. She does not say much—hardly anything at all—and takes little active part in Job's journey after her short speech.[10] The little she does say is quite ambiguous:

ותאמר לו אשתו ערך מחזיק בתמתך ברך אלהים ומת

Do you still persist in your integrity?[11] Bless God, and die.

The basic thrust of these words is not clear. The majority voice in tradition[12] has interpreted them *ad malem partem* and consequently demonized their speaker. Verse 9bα is understood as a mocking question: "Are you still holding onto your strength?" Job's wife is seen as mocking her

meinem Fleische werde ich meinen Gott schauen." Die späteren abendländischen Übersetzungen (Luther, AV, StV u.a.) sind hiervon stark beeinflusst und bieten ähnliche Wiedergaben dieser Verse; b) Hiob erwartet, nach seinem Tode im Totenreich gerechtfertigt zu werden (Ewald, Dillmann, Weiser, N. H. Ridderbos, Kroeze); c) Hiob erwartet, dass Gott von seiner Gerechtigkeit nach dem Tode vor den Menschen Zeugnis ablegen wird (Hölscher, Streeder); d) Hiob erwartet, dass er als Geist aus der Erde steigen wird (etwa wie Samuel 1 Sam 28) und eben als Geist Gott selber sehen wird; dieser wird dann ein Zeichen, z.B. an seinem Grabe, geben, um Hiob zu rechtfertigen (Duhm). Wir wenden ein: wider (a): Der Glaube an Auferstehung meldet sich in Israel erst im zweiten Jahrhundert v. Chr., vgl. Dan 1,22 II Makk 7,14 Sap 1,15; 3,5.23; Jes 26,19; wider (b): Hier wird eine Darstellung von Scheol vorausgesetzt, die nicht zu den anderen Aussagen Hiobs über den Zustand im Totenreich passt; wider (c): Dies würde dem Hiob im Totenreich keine Genugtuung geben, vgl. 14,21; wider (d): Hiobs Überzeugung ist, dass einer, der zum Totenreich niedergestiegen ist, nicht wiederkehrt, s. 9,9f.; 10,21; 14,12.18ff.; 16,22; 17,13.]

9. See the excellent analysis by M. Witte, "'Aber Gott wird meine Seele erlösen'—Tod und Leben nach Psalm XLIX," *VT* 50 (2000) 540–60.

10. The text on one occasion states that Job's breath (or spirit) has become strange to her (19:17); most translators exaggerate this statement by reading it as "My breath is loathsome to my wife." Job's children, who are returned to him in 42:13, seem to be born without the involvement of a woman: "And seven sons and three daughters were made to him." Traditional exegesis has connected this odd phrase with a particular interpretation: because his wife had tempted Job to curse God, she died before his restitution. His new children (42:13–15) are thus born from a new wife.

11. Verse 9a is almost always treated as a question. In Hebrew, a question does not have to be indicated by an interrogative particle according to *GKC* §150a. But neither is a statement indicated by the lack of an interrogative particle!

12. See Z. Gitay, "The Portrayal of Job's Wife and Her Representation in the Visual Arts," in *Fortunate the Eyes That See* (ed. A. B. Beck; Grand Rapids: Eerdmans, 1995) 516–26.

husband—she is the female analogue to the *satan* in 2:5—an *adiuvatrix diaboli*. She mocks his faith, which in the end did not prove to be the foundation he believed it to be. She encourages him to commit suicide by blaspheming God so harshly that it would cause his own death.

It is, however, also possible to interpret these words *ad bonam partem*[13] by reading them as analogy to God's statement in 2:3b. Taking ברך literally as 'blessing', not as a euphemism for 'cursing',[14] we could paraphrase:

> Job, I admire that you can still hold on to your faith despite all that has befallen you. But I advise you: Make peace with God because your end is near and desirable. Give up![15]

---

13. See M. Cheney, *Dust, Wind and Agony: Character, Speech and Genre in Job* (ConBOT 39; Stockholm: Almquist & Wiksell, 1994) 76; C. Maier and S. Schroer, "Das Buch Ijob," in *Kompendium feministischer Bibelauslegung* (ed. L. Schottroff and M.-T. Wacker; Gütersloh 1998) 192–207 (esp. 201–3).

14. D. O'Connor, "'Bless God and Die (Job 2:9): Euphemism or Irony?" *PIBA* 19 (1996) 48–65.

15. This tendency is also expressed in G. Fohrer, *Das Buch Hiob* (KAT 16; Gütersloh: Gütersloher, 1988) 102–3:

> The narrative makes use of the experience that the woman is anchored more strongly in the realm of emotions and acts in unmediated fashion out of this impulse. Differently from the man, she sees the desperation and inescapability of the situation. This stirs up her question about why Job holds fast to his integrity, and her advice to curse God and die. . . . While the *satan*'s only interest was to demonstrate the selfishness and self-interest of the piety of the servant praised by God, the woman actually attempts to get him to give it up. This has to do with what remains for Job after the loss of his possessions and his health: his piety and his life. Differently from Job, his wife evidently assumes that belief in God must bring humans some kind of benefit. When Job loses his possessions and health, then his piety is revealed as useless. Therefore, it would be best for him to give it up in order that, as a consequence, an end to the entire ordeal would be accomplished. Then the advice of the woman would be seen as temporal: "Relieve your heart by cursing before you die!" This would be trivial rather than tempting; in addition, this understanding is grammatically unlikely. The advice should be understood as telic: "Curse God so that as a result of it death will quickly follow and you be liberated from your suffering!" It is the expression of complete desperation and hopelessness that stand behind the simultaneous concern and empathy for the tortured man whom no one can help.

> [Die Erzählung bedient sich dazu der Erfahrung, dass die Frau stärker im Gefühlsleben wurzelt und unmittelbarer aus ihm handelt. Anders als der Mann sieht sie das Verzweifelte und Unausweichliche der Lage. Daraus rühren ihre Frage, warum Hiob an seiner Lauterkeit festhalte, und ihr Rat, Gott zu fluchen und zu sterben. . . . Während es dem Satan nur darum ging, die Selbstsucht und den Eigennutz der Frömmigkeit des von Gott gelobten Knechtes nachzuweisen, sucht die Frau ihn zu deren Aufgaben überhaupt zu bewegen. Es geht um das, was Hiob nach dem Verlust seines Besitzes und seiner Gesundheit geblieben ist: seine Frömmigkeit und sein Leben. Anders als er selbst geht die Frau offenbar davon aus, dass der Gottesglaube dem Menschen irgendeinen Nutzen bringen muß. Wenn Hiob nun Besitz und Gesundheit verloren hat, ist seine Frömmigkeit als nutzlos erwiesen. Dann ist es am besten, sie ganz aufzugeben, damit als Folge dessen wie-

Job's harsh rejection of her words ("you are talking like a foolish woman"; v. 10) would then refer to her advice to give up and accept death (by committing suicide?). Job rejects this cowardice with a kind of heroic optimism, believing that everything has its meaning, that suffering must be endured, and that only fools escape by seeking death.

In the Septuagint, Job's wife presents a much longer speech:

[2:9] Χρόνου δὲ πολλοῦ προβεβηκότος εἶπεν αὐτῷ ἡ γυνὴ αὐτοῦ Μέχρι τίνος καρτερήσεις λέγων [9a] Ἰδοὺ ἀναμένω χρόνον ἔτι μικρὸν προσδεχόμενος τὴν ἐλπίδα τῆς σωτηρίας μου; [9b] ἰδοὺ γὰρ ἠφάνισταί σου τὸ μνημόσυνον ἀπὸ τῆς γῆς, υἱοὶ καὶ θυγατέρες, ἐμῆς κοιλίας ὠδῖνες καὶ πόνοι, οὓς εἰς τὸ κενὸν ἐκοπίασα μετὰ μόχθων. [9c] σύ τε αὐτὸς ἐν σαπρίᾳ σκωλήκων κάθησαι διανυκτερεύων αἴθριος· [9d] κἀγὼ πλανῆτις καὶ λάτρις τόπον ἐκ τόπου περιερχομένη καὶ οἰκίαν ἐξ οἰκίας προσδεχομένη τὸν ἥλιον πότε δύσεται, ἵνα ἀναπαύσωμαι τῶν μόχθων καὶ τῶν ὀδυνῶν, αἵ με νῦν συνέχουσιν. [9e] ἀλλὰ εἰπόν τι ῥῆμα εἰς κύριον καὶ τελεύτα.

Then, after a long time had passed, his wife said to him, "How long will you persist and say, 'Look, I will hang on a little longer, while I wait for the hope of my deliverance?' For look, your legacy has vanished from the earth—*even your* sons and daughters, my womb's birth pangs and labors, for whom I wearied myself with hardships in vain. And you? You sit in the refuse of worms as you spend the night in the open air. As for me, I am one that wanders about and a hired servant—from place to place and house to house, waiting for when the sun will set, so that I may rest from the distresses and griefs that now beset me. Now say some word to the Lord, and die!"

According to this text, quoted almost verbatim in *Testament of Job* 23, a pseudepigraphic writing of the first century c.e., the wife is the one who initiates the lament by crying out: "How long?" In moving terms, she describes the loss of her children as the loss of her future, as the annulment of all her labor. She describes the burden of losing her social standing[16]

der der ganzen Qual ein Ende gesetzt wird. Denn der Rat der Frau ist keinesfalls zeitlich zu verstehen: Erleichtere dir dein Herz durch Fluchen, bevor du stirbst! Das wäre trivial und nicht versucherisch; zudem ist diese Auffassung grammatisch unwahrscheinlich. Der Rat ist final zu verstehen: Fluche Gott, damit du durch den deswegen folgenden Tod bald von deinem Leiden befreit wirst! Es ist ein Ausdruck völliger Verzweiflung und Hoffnungslosigkeit, hinter dem gleichzeitig Sorge und Mitleid für den gequälten Mann stehen, dem niemand helfen kann.]

16. This portrait of a wife who, like "Mother Courage" fights for her sick husband and her own survival, is strongly reminiscent of Hannah in Tobit 2.

and the desire to escape her pain (it could be that the image of the "setting sun" is a euphemism for death as a welcome friend). She stands at Job's side as one who suffers with him. I can find no fault with this kind of counseling. Job's wife becomes the one who voices his lament and thus proves to be a trusted companion. Even if Job pushes her back and tries to silence her with standard theological phrases, he will eventually take up his wife's lament and expand it greatly. He will speak of his economic and societal suffering (especially in chap. 30) and beg for release from his pain. I believe that the long tradition depicting Job's wife as an *adiuvatrix diaboli*, an aid to the devil,[17] needs to be corrected. The text is not so clear. We must take its ambiguities seriously.[18]

3. The Counseling Strategies of Job's Friends

Job's friends, who respond to his inner and outer distress and come to his aid, try many different approaches to remind the suffering friend of God and of his (former) relationship to him—all in the attempt to alleviate his misery. As in the case of Job's wife, reception history has treated them very poorly: they are considered the personification of empty phrases; they are horrible comforters who are unable to see the actual suffering of the person in front of them; they are only interested in defending a certain dogma of God. I do not believe that this negative interpretation is substantiated by the text. I believe the long poems portray them as good friends and true counselors. The following factors support this view.

1. In their *silent presence*, they show a high degree of solidarity. This is already quite an achievement! (One important aspect of counseling, however, seems to me to be missing: physical contact. Or was Job too unclean due to his illness to be held or caressed? Why do the friends not cry with him? We hear of such crying only in Job 2:12. After that, they seem emotionally distant.)

2. The friends are able to *wait* for seven long days[19] to hear what Job has to say for himself. The have the gift of *listening*. At the beginning of his speech, Eliphaz shows a great deal of reticence and compassion (Job 4:1–4).

---

17. An off-color joke remarks: "Why did God not also take Job's wife? Because he wanted to return everything twofold in the end."

18. Cf. C. L. Seow, "Job's Wife, with Due Respect," in *Das Buch Hiob und seine Interpretationen: Beiträge zum Hiob-Symposiums auf dem Monte Verità vom 14.–19. August 2005,* ed. Thomas Krüger et al. (ATANT 88; Zurich: TVZ 2007), 351–73.

19. I do not believe a reference to the *Shiva* silence of Jewish tradition to be a very likely explanation of this time.

3. They are not just "mirrors" or "amplifiers" of Job's suffering, their *counseling includes objection*. This "oppositional poimenics" takes shape

(3a) in their *reminder of Job's own former theological beliefs*, held by him in happier days (see Job 4:3–6):

See, you have instructed many; you have strengthened the weak hands. Your words have supported those who were stumbling, and you have made firm the feeble knees. But now it has come to you, and you are impatient; it touches you, and you are dismayed. Is not your fear of God your confidence, and the integrity of your ways your hope?

(3b) in *reference to the promises of God*, which now seem to be contradicted by Job's experience. Job's friends uphold these promises against Job's experience:

If you direct your heart rightly, you will stretch out your hands toward him. . . . And your life will be brighter than the noonday; its darkness will be like the morning. (Job 11:13, 17)

If you return to the Almighty, you will be restored, if you remove unrighteousness from your tents. (Job 22:23)

(3c) as *anamnesis* of long-held beliefs obscured by current misery, as reminder of *commonly held wisdom principles* such as the theological theory of suffering as divine pedagogy (Job 5:17–18; 35);

(3d) and as application of the belief in a just causal connection between action and consequence, even if this leads to personal attacks such as "You must have sinned." Job is given the freedom to figure out what this sin may have consisted of. Job's friends do not accuse him immediately of concrete misdeeds; they merely open up a space that allows Job to stand alone with his personal guilt. The friends confront him with *direct accusations of misdeeds* only after he proves unable or unwilling to enter this intimate space of personal guilt.

Is not your wickedness great? There is no end to your iniquities. For you have exacted pledges from your family for no reason, and stripped the naked of their clothing. You have given no water to the weary to drink, and you have withheld bread from the hungry. The powerful possess the land, and the favored live in it. You have sent widows away empty-handed, and the arms of the orphans you have crushed. Therefore snares are around you, and sudden terror overwhelms you. (Job 22:5–10)

This direct accusation has been subjected again and again to harsh criticism. But it is of high importance as a "fundamental starting point in counseling." Nathan's parable in 2 Sam 12:1–4 is a model for such counseling. It leads David to the insight: "You are the man!" By enabling the perpetrator to accept his guilt, he is led to confession and remorse *following which* God's forgiveness is once again bestowed upon him!

(3e) Elihu makes his own contribution as a counselor, at least as I understand him: in Job 33, he shows how God's grace comes as a pure *gift of grace*, brought on through the intercessory prayer of an angel. This theological concept strengthens our hope that the suffering sinner also remains in the embrace of the powers of heaven.

The concept that God educates human beings through suffering, that Job's illness is a constructive didactic measure, has moved to the center of much recent scholarship on Job.[20] Yet there is much that speaks against advocating such pedagogy of suffering. Even if the Greek proverb that opens Goethe's autobiography states that only a tried and tested individual can become a truly educated individual, the idea that God deliberately brings about suffering so that certain individuals may grow in maturity is more masochistic than sarcastic, nor is it justified by the text.

(3f) One of Elihu's central themes is *creation theology*. Demonstrating God's power and might is an important source for counseling: it is intended to strengthen Job's trust in a just world order. The full complexity of this order may not be fully understandable, but its grandeur points to a well-organized structure. Elihu even prefigures God's answer to Job in chapters 38–41, especially in his final speech in chapters 36–37.

4. God's Counseling Strategy

Every reader of the book of Job is gripped by the tension created by the question of how Yahweh is going to respond to Job, whose suffering was directly caused by him. At first, however, the book only conveys God's silence. It takes a long time before Job receives an answer from God. Job already despairs that God will ever respond to him. Even following his final exasperation in chapter 31 ("Shaddai, answer me!" v. 35), he encoun-

---

20. See T. Mende, *Durch Leiden zur Vollendung: Die Elihureden im Buch Ijob* (TThSt 49; Trier: Paulinus-Verlag, 1991); H.-M. Wahl, *Der gerechte Schöpfer: Eine redaktions- und theologiegeschichtliche Untersuchung der Elihureden—Hiob 32–37* (BZAW 207; Berlin: de Gruyter, 1993).

ters nothing but silence. Instead of hearing from God, a fourth friend appears. Just like Abraham, who had resigned in his old age ("Lord Yahweh, what can you give me?" Gen 15:2), Job must wait.

Yahweh finally does appear "in a storm" and gives a long speech. The interpretation of what he actually says is a matter of intense debate.

Even the text of Job 38–42:6 itself is fraught with difficulties: these include the double or even triple introductions to separate speeches (38:1; 40:1, 6; see also 42:7) and Job's two-fold answer. These repetitions raise the suspicion that the text may not be an original unit but rather the result of a complicated process of textual growth.[21] The subsequent interpretations are highly dependent on the diachronic decisions made in this context. I would like briefly to present only seven important suggestions:

1. One group of scholars believes that what God says is not important. The only pertinent fact is that *he speaks to Job at all.* Job's lament is transformed by an encounter with the living God.[22]

Most scholars, however, believe that the specific content of the divine monologues is of decisive importance. What this importance may be, however, varies greatly:

2. God intended to silence Job. He rebukes him and rejects him with a highly questionable demonstration of his eternal superiority. Nevertheless, in all his boasting, God is not able to hide the fact that he is merely making excuses. In this view, the divine monologues are a *subtle critique of religion.*

3. God says nothing different from what the friends had already said. This is especially true for Elihu (Job 36–37). All of the rumblings of weather and storm is nothing other than a dramatic *performance.* In this view, the book is a satire written for the purpose of entertainment.

4. The divine speeches are examples of *skeptical wisdom*; they demonstrate the failure of wisdom to understand the ultimate questions of existence.

5. The divine speeches show that creation mirrors the positive aspects of God. Reflection on the subtleties of a life-giving and live-sustaining order of things leads to a strengthening of faith in God's incomprehensible plan. Even undeserved suffering is thus a result of his love and friendship and serves a higher end.

---

21. For an overview of proposed composition-critical solutions, see J. van Oorschot, *Gott als Grenze: Eine literar- und redaktionsgeschichtliche Studie zu den Gottesreden des Hiobbuches* (BZAW 170; Berlin: de Gruyter, 1987).

22. E.g., T. Veijola, "Offenbarung als Begegnung: Von der Möglichkeit einer Theologie des Alten Testaments," *ZTK* 88 (1991) 427–50.

6. An analysis of the iconography of the ancient Near East shows that the divine speeches contain images associated with the "Lord of the animals." In this view, God is intent on constraining chaotic and life-threatening elements in this world that still enjoy a certain amount of autonomy. The divine speeches answer Job's lament with a proto-apocalyptic and dualistic world view that depicts God in constant battle with the forces of chaos for the good of humanity. This battle demands much from God and also includes setbacks.

7. In connection with this view, several scholars suggest that Yahweh intends to admonish Job to shoulder his own part in the battle against evil.

8. One last suggestion tries to show that the divine monologues intend to show Job that God does not care *only* for human beings. God is concerned with the greater good. Job needs to learn that a "meta-order" exists beyond the order of the human world; it, too, is the focus of God's concern and care. Job's anthropocentric world view is transformed by showing Job the larger contexts in which he exists.

This last suggestion comes closest to the original intention of the text: creation theology is accorded significant counseling potential. With this I do not mean that God strengthens Job's optimistic faith in the order and harmony of things; Job's fate is not shown to be meaningful in the end. The intent of God's speech is to confront Job with a *healthy disappointment*: "Who are you? How important do you think you are? You are merely a small drop of time in the eternal ocean of the world. God's answer is thus quite surprising. The Priestly writings in Genesis 1 still advocated an optimistic anthropocentrism in their view of creation. Psalm 8 marveled at the divinely bestowed human dignity and the authority of *homo faber*. The book of Job, however, takes a different position: Yahweh's speech communicates to Job that he is not as important for God's overall plan as he may have believed. Chapters 38–42 provide us with a theological counterbalance that surprises all participants in the "case study" of Job.

5. The Question of Relevance: Can Biblical Strategies of Poimenics be Applied Constructively to Our World Today?

In current discussions of pastoral theology,[23] we encounter several different programmatic approaches to the reception of biblical models.[24]

---

23. Cf. on this C. Möller, *Examensreader für Praktische Theologie* (11th ed.; Heidelberg: self-published, 1995) 182–241.

24. In addition to the literature mentioned in n. 1, cf. H. Tacke, *Mit den Müden zur rechten Zeit reden: Beiträge zu einer bibelorientierten Seelsorge* (Neukirchen-Vluyn: Neukirchener Verlag, 1989).

On the whole, it has become clear that pastoral psychology has come to replace kerygmatic answers. How do we position the various strategies in book of Job within the current discussion? [25]

1. Job's own strategy will probably find the greatest number of supporters. Job's basic view that he does not deserve his suffering is widespread. Many people believe that suffering, especially their own suffering, is a form of injustice in and of itself. Even if the proclamations of innocence today are most often less radical than in the case of Job, many suffer from the basic feeling: "I am basically alright. There is nothing I did that might have justified this. Why is God punishing me?"[26] Most often, the counselor is confronted with the basic existential question: "Why?" Most people do not actually expect an answer to this "Why?" because they believe that they are innocent and undeserving of their fate. The counselor could make no worse mistake than suggesting a reason or reasons to explain the suffering. In Job, who again and again confronts God and upholds his blamelessness, I recognize a seminal model for current pastoral care.

2. The friends are criticized harshly. They are seen as representatives of empty and insensitive theological dogmatism.[27] But they are better than their reputation. Despite their patient waiting, Job's comforters are not ancient predecessors of Carl Rogers; they do not practice client-centered counseling. By asking critical questions on the basis of their theological tradition, they are role models of kerygmatic pastoral theology who try to convince a suffering individual by means of the sufferer's own theological beliefs; pastoral care must also include this component of theological discourse. The friends are not looking for "merciful lies" that may provide short term emotional solace; they do not succumb to "easy truths"

---

25. In the 6½ years that I worked as a hospital chaplain, I was continually confronted with this existential question. I imagine that I might encounter an individual in his hospital bed who suffers physically and spiritually. His outer appearance evokes pity—his skin is full of festering sores—and he speaks to me in a weak and bitter voice and tells me of his life. He used to be on the top, healthy, and well respected in his family and community. Now he has fallen into the depths and has lost everything—his money, his family, and his health. Everything has fallen apart. His upsetting life story ends in uncanny silence. According to current pastoral theology, how am I supposed to approach this person? How is he supposed to deal with his loss and feelings?

26. Feminist theology especially has declared its intent to make high self-esteem the foundation for theological anthropology; see, e.g., E. Moltmann-Wendel, "Opfer oder Hingabe – Sühnopfer oder Gottesfreundschaft?" in *Sühne-Opfer-Abendmahl* (ed. A. Wagner; Neukirchen-Vluyn: Neukirchener Verlag, 1999) 63–77.

27. Even J. Ebach, who at first protects the friends and views their theological approach to Job's problem as appropriate, finally reproaches them for spiritual intransigence; cf. Ebach, "Gott und die Normativität des Faktischen: Ein Plädoyer für die Freunde Hiobs," in *Hiobs Post* (ed. J. Ebach; Neukirchen-Vluyn: Neukirchener Verlag, 1995) 55–66.

that fail to be relevant and stable in the long run (such as: "The world is good"). They confront Job with a complex view of God, who can also appear as a stern judge and who expects human beings to take their proper place, subordinate to him. Their pastoral care is a guide to repentance. That the friends dare to refer back to possible sins, based on Job's fate, has often been criticized. This audacity, however, is a basic reflex in many Old Testament texts: the barrenness of women (Gen 20), Achan's theft (Judg 7), David's census (2 Sam 24), and the storm in the book of Jonah (Jonah 1). The fact that the friends interpret Job's experience by way of analogy to the paradigmatic stories of their tradition is not an immediate reason to reject their efforts as "ideology." The attitude that suffering and sin may actually be connected is found in many parts of the Old Testament,[28] even if it has become taboo for many contemporary counselors.

3. God's answer has had a particularly hard time in contemporary counseling theory. Human individuals are no more than a speck of dust in a huge cosmos not created for their benefit? That is all? Yet I believe that this answer previews insights from modern psychology:

> Over time, the sciences have caused human beings to suffer two major put-downs of their naive self love. The first occurred when they discovered that the earth is not at the center of the universe, but merely a *tiny particle in an unimaginably large system.* This put-down is connected with the name of Copernicus, even if science under Alexander the Great had already made similar statements. The second came when Biology destroyed *the imagined priority of humans in creation* and pointed to their continuity to the animal kingdom and the inescapability of their animal nature. This paradigm shift has happened in our times under the influence of C. Darwin, Wallace, and their predecessors and has encountered severe opposition from their contemporaries. A third and most severe put-down is awaiting human illusions of grandeur from Psychology. I intend to show that the individual is not even lord of his own manor but is dependent on sparse information from what is happening unconsciously in his soul. We psychoanalytics are also not the first and the only ones to point out the necessity of this reflection, but it seems that we are given the

---

28. M. Oeming " 'Mein Herz ist durchbohrt in meinem Innern' (Ps 109,22): Krankheit und Leid in alttestamentlicher Sicht," in *Krankheit und Leid in der Sicht der Religionen* (ed. M. Oeming; Osnabrück: Univ., Fachbereich Erziehungs- und Kulturwissenschaft, 1994) 3–28.

role of proclaiming it in most urgent terms. . . . This is why our science is met with such opposition.[29]

Just as the heliocentric worldview robbed human beings of their central status, just as the theory of genetic origin robbed human beings of his genetic uniqueness, and as psychoanalysis destroyed humanity's illusions of rationality, God's answer contradicts Job's ideas of his own position and importance. This is also the reason why this text has encountered so much opposition. God's put-down may not be his last word in the book (see 42:7), but it is an important and healthy proclamation that can solve many problems. I am not surprised that this approach is missing in all of the textbooks on pastoral care that I have read. If the friends have already provoked opposition, this is even true for God's approach to counseling in the book of Job. Nonetheless, a counselor should not always say what the listeners want to hear; he must also speak the truth.

The book of Job is no doubt lacking several important aspects of pastoral theology: we hear nothing of the fact that suffering creates solidarity among those who suffer, or that human beings can mature and become a more positive part of society after going through pain and guilt; there is also no indication of a life to come, of God's world to come. Despite all this, I believe the book of Job to be an important poimenical treatise that should be given stronger emphasis in current discussions.

---

29. S. Freud, "Vorlesungen zur Einführung in die Psychoanalyse (1916/17)," *Studienausgabe* (12th ed.; Frankfurt a.M.: Fischer, 1994) 1:283–84:

> Zwei große Kränkungen ihrer naiven Eigenliebe hat die Menschheit im Laufe der Zeiten von der Wissenschaft erdulden müssen. Die erste, als sie erfuhr, daß unsere Erde nicht der Mittelpunkt des Weltalls ist, sondern *ein winziges Teilchen eines in seiner Größe kaum vorstellbaren Weltsystems.* Sie knüpft sich für uns an den Namen Kopernikus, obwohl schon die alexandrinische Wissenschaft ähnliches verkündet hatte. Die zweite dann, als die biologische Forschung *das angebliche Schöpfungsvorrecht* des Menschen zunichte machte, ihn auf die Abstammung aus dem Tierreich und die Unvertilgbarkeit seiner animalischen Natur verweis. Diese Umwertung hat sich in unseren Tagen unter dem Einfluß von Ch. Darwin, Wallace und ihren Vorgängern nicht ohne das heftigste Sträuben der Zeitgenossen vollzogen. Die dritte und empfindlichste Kränkung aber soll die menschliche Größensucht durch die heutige psychologische Forschung erfahren, welche dem Ich nachweisen will, daß nicht einmal Herr im eigenen Hause, sondern auf kärgliche Nachrichten angewiesen bleibt von dem, was unbewußt in seinem Seelenleben vorgeht. Auch diese Mahnung zur Einkehr haben wir Psychoanalytiker nicht zuerst und nicht als einzige vorgetragen, aber es scheint uns beschieden, sie am eindringlichsten zu vertreten. . . . Daher die allgemeine Auflehnung gegen unsere Wissenschaft.

The emphasis is mine to demonstrate the connection to Job.

CHAPTER 3

Job's Monologue: A Journey Inward

MANFRED OEMING

1. Job 31 as an Answer to His Friends

The dialogues come to an end, and finally three monologues start (Job, Elihu, God). Job is first, in Job 29–31.[1] In chapter 31, we encounter the final climax of Job's argument with his friends. They had tried to rebuke him first with insinuations and then with open accusations. They admonished him to stop diminishing, repressing, and disavowing his guilt. His suffering was not brought on without reason. Job is called to entertain the thought that his suffering may be just punishment; in acknowledging his sin, he holds the key to understanding his fate. His hubris against God must be seen as highly problematic and his insistence on his own innocence a sign of profound moral aberration against his creator. His claims to innocence neglect two major details: sins of omission and structural entanglement in violence.[2] Job has not done everything in his power to aid individuals in need; instead, he has accepted the consequences of "capitalism" without protest. He has fallen short of the radical criteria of God that are embodied in the ethical statements of the prophets. He never entertained the idea of radically upsetting the harsh laws of a market economy.

---

1. Cf. the detailed analysis by D. Opel, *Hiobs Anspruch und Widerspruch: Die Herausforderungsreden Hiobs (Hi 29–31) im Kontext frühjüdischer Ethik* (WMANT 127; Neukirchen-Vluyn: Neukirchener Verlag, 2010), who explains the role and the ethics of Job against a typical royal background.

2. Most often, interpreters evaluate the friends' accusations as inflexible dogmatism. Because they are unable to point to specific misdeeds, they arbitrarily accuse him of the worst crimes. This interpretation remains problematic because it accuses the friends a priori of being intellectually lazy and theologically incompetent.

Is not your wickedness great? There is no end to your iniquities. For you have exacted pledges from your family for no reason, and stripped them naked of their clothing. You have given no water to the weary to drink, and you have withheld bread from the hungry. The powerful possess the land, and the favored live in it. You have sent widows away empty-handed, and the arms of the orphans you have crushed. Therefore snares are around you, and sudden terror overwhelms you. (Job 22:5–10)

In refutation of these accusations, Job presents his view of things in a final speech that is designed to prove his innocence. He can only think of punishment in a *modus irrealis*. This or that *would be* worthy of punishment, but he has been guilty of none of it. He passionately fights for recognition of the fact that he has done absolutely nothing to deserve God's harsh punishment. He goes through his life story in detail, surveying the long period of blessing and the period of suffering (Job 29–30). He examines his own conscience by reflecting on the motives that were characteristic of his thoughts and deeds. Considered just in terms of its length, Job 31 is a unique piece of life reflection and introspection in the Old Testament. In this introspection, Job reflects on the main accusations of his possible crimes and concludes in each instance that his conscience is clean. The preeminent form of this self-analysis is the limited self-curse in combination with an oath:[3] "I have certainly not committed this or that crime." The following chapter presents an analysis of this cleansing of the heart.

Job begins (vv. 1–12) by insisting that he never looked desiringly at a young woman. Is lust of the eyes seen here as the most fundamental of all sins that leads to all other misdeeds? This does indeed seem surprising. Many interpreters thus already view this first statement as problematic: as many modern and rabbinic Jewish interpreters point out, elsewhere in the Old Testament, merely looking at young women is only seen as foolish, not as sinful (Sir 9:5). Some scholars see in this text a secondary addition or suggest changes in its wording;[4] others imagine that the statement

---

3. "(I shall be accursed) if I have done this or that." The widespread interpretation of the אם-clauses as protasis that are followed irregularly by an apodosis (see G. Fohrer, *Das Buch Hiob* [KAT 16; Gütersloh: Gütersloher, 1988] and A de Wilde, *Das Buch Hiob* [OTS 22; Leiden: Brill 1981]) ignores this possibility. On the form of the elliptic oath, its tense, and other problematic issues see *GKC* § 149b, c.

4. S. R. Driver and G. B. Gray, *A Critical and Exegetical Commentary on the Book of Job Together with a New Translation* (ICC; Edinburgh: T. & T. Clark, 1921) suggests that we read נְבָלָה ("godlessness") instead of בְּתוּלָה ("young woman").

refers to a *heavenly* young woman such as the goddess Anat.[5] All this is
quite unlikely. We are dealing with a unique passage in the Old Testament
where lustful eyes are seen as the root of all evil. The connection to the 7th
and the 10th commandments of the Decalogue is obvious. Equally clear
is the radicalization of these commandments. We must also note the harsh
punishment that follows this desire. From misery and bad fortune in v. 3,
the text escalates to the loss of harvest in v. 8, the loss of one's wife in v. 10,
up to burning fire in v. 12 that destroys everything down to its foundations. It appears that, in this late period of Old Testament literature, the
family is placed under special protection. Invading and destroying another
family is out of the question. Abstinence in the face of tempting "young
women," the renunciation of lying and cheating (connected directly to
adultery), marital fidelity, and respect for the family of one's neighbor—all
these are the virtues that Job affirms for himself first of all.

These observations allow certain deductions about the sociohistorical
context of the text.

1. The basic unit of the Postexilic Period is the clan, the בֵּית אָבִי
   'house of the father'.[6] This unit is defended at all costs. It seems
   that such defense was also necessary, as the repeated warnings
   show.
2. The place and the dignity of women is continually elevated,
   despite remaining androcentric limitations. Even the wealthy
   individual should not lust after young women. At first glance,
   v. 10 does not seem to fit with the argument; it is a monstrosity
   to place the punishment for adultery on the cheated wife. The
   text, however, seems to be intended as a warning, indicating that
   an adulterous husband will lose his wife to dishonor.
3. Without mentioning it explicitly, the text seems to assume an
   ideal of monogamy behind the statements in vv. 1–12. We can see
   this mainly in the singular "my wife" in v. 10.

The topic of verses 13–15 is legal argument. An intensified version of
the ninth commandment provides the background for these statements:
Job not only engaged in fair legal discourse with social equals but also
with his own "staff." He treated his socially inferior male and female ser-

---

5. A. R. Ceresco, "Job 29–31 in the Light of Northwest Semitic," *BO* 36 (1980)
107f; W. L. Michel, "BTWLH, 'Virgin', or 'Virgin (Anat)' in Job 31:1," *HS* 23 (1982)
59–66 and others.

6. Cf. R. Albertz, *Vom Exil bis zu den Makkabäern*, vol. 2 of *Religionsgeschichte Israels
in Alttestamentlicher Zeit* (ATD Ergänzung 8/2; Göttingen: Vandenhoeck & Ruprecht,
1992) 473–74, 608.

vants with equal respect. Two concepts provide the context for this action: For one, it refers back to the insight—often reiterated in prophetic and wisdom literature as well as in the Psalms—that God will further the cause of the *personae miserae* (v. 14; see also Prov 22:22–23: "Do not rob the poor because they are poor, or crush the afflicted at the gate; for the LORD pleads their cause and despoils of life those who despoil them.") Second—and this is of high importance—the text provides an argument on the basis of creation theology: both lord and servant are created by one and the same God (v. 15). We may read this as an early anticipation of Gal 3:28: In Shaddai, there is no lord or servant, no man nor woman. They are all created by the One. There are at most three other passages in Old Testament that at least partially reflect this attitude: "Have we not all one father? Has not one God created us? Why then are we faithless to one another, profaning the covenant of our ancestors?" (Mal 2:10);[7] "The rich and the poor have this in common: the LORD is the maker of them all" (Prov 22:2); "Those who mock the poor insult their Maker; those who are glad at calamity will not go unpunished" (Prov 17:5). In vv. 16–23, Job describes his dealings with socially weak groups—with the poor, the widows and orphans, the naked, and the innocent.[8] There is no commandment in the Decalogue that provides a background for these statements. Job has done much more than the law demands. He has even complied with the high demand of the prophets for increased protection of the poor and the weak. He has used his financial position to show a considerable degree of social solidarity. Once again, the text resorts to explicit theological explanations: v. 18 (despite its problematic textual issues) refers back to the blessings Job himself received from God.[9] It also mentions the ruin that lies in God's judgment, here symbolized in tearing arms out of their sockets (vv. 22–23).

The text further poetically combines the power of gleaming money and the twinkling of the stars in vv. 24–28. Job was not tempted by either source of light. His wealth did not tempt him to believe in himself or his own power, and the stars did not tempt him to intimate adoration—indicated

---

7. In this context, the statement refers to mixed marriages and divorce so that we have to especially emphasize the "us" in "Has God not created us?"

8. This list bears strong resemblance to Eliphaz's accusations in 22:1–4. Here we see a clear indication that Job's monologue in chap. 31 is a continuation of the dialogue with his friends.

9. "From my youth, God has raised me as a father. He has led me from the bosom of my mother." According to a rare textual variant of the MT, the verse indicates that Job acted as a father figure ever since his childhood: "Ever since my youth, the orphan grew up with me as a father, I led him from the bosom of my mother."

here as "secret kisses."[10] Job has kept the first and second commandment
in his heart and in secret. He did not bow down to mammon or the stars;
he did not imbue them with divine dignity and worship them. He knows
well that this would be a punishable sin.

Another remarkable aspect of Job's introspection is his attitude toward
those who hate him in vv. 29–30. In a very few select instances, Torah and
wisdom literature also admonish the individual to maintain moderation
toward enemies,[11] but most often in order to put them to shame. It also
seems that these passages are limited to members of one's own people.
The most closely related text is Prov 24:17: "Do not rejoice when your
enemies fall, and do not let your heart be glad when they stumble," yet
here also with the concluding statement: "or else the LORD will see it
and be displeased, and turn away his anger from them." Such a statement
is missing in Job 31:29–30. Job refers back to the third commandment
and defines the curse against and the death wish placed on enemies as sin
(quite in contrast to many statements in the Psalms). This makes Job 31 a
very unique text in the Old Testament, perhaps superseded only by 2 Chr
28:15, where the victorious inhabitants of the North, following a command by the prophet Oded, clothe their vanquished foes, provide them
with something to drink, anoint them, seat them on donkeys, and guide
them home. This Old Testament version of the Samaritan is also an important text for Jewish ethics in the late Persian and early Hellenistic eras.[12]

Once again (compare vv. 16–23), Job emphasizes his generosity, now
embodied in the luxurious food that he offers traveling strangers. Hospitality is a high virtue in the ancient Near East, especially among nomads.

Job's integrity and the high social standing that he so eloquently describes in chapter 29 is not based on illusion and falsehood. It may be human nature to conceal one's failings in public, but Job is bold enough to
stand trial even "in the face of the people" (vv. 33–34; see Sir 1:29). We
are reminded of the 9th commandment. In this context, however, it is ap-

10. This is what is meant by the expression: "my mouth has kissed my hand."

11. Exod 23:4–5 (come to the aid of the enemy's donkey); Lev 19:18 (prohibition
of taking revenge on members of one's people), see H.-P. Mathys, *Liebe deinen Nächsten
wie dich selbst: Untersuchungen zum alttestamentlichen Gebot der Nächstenliebe (Lev 19, 18)*
(2nd ed.; OBO 71; Freiburg, Schweiz: Universitätsverlag and Göttingen: Vandenhoeck &
Ruprecht, 1990); Prov 20:22 (Do not retaliate in evil against your enemy. God will come to
your aid); 24:17 (Do not rejoice over the fall of your enemy.); 25:21–22 (feed the hungry
enemy as heap burning coals on his head); see A. Meinhold, "Der Umgang mit dem Feind
nach Spr 25,21f. als Maßstab für das Menschsein," in *Alttestamentlicher Glaube und Biblische
Theologie* (ed. J. Hausmann and H.-J. Zobel; Stuttgart: Kohlhammer, 1992) 244–52; Sir
3:16 [Hebr.] ("Whoever oppresses the weak or curses father or mother mocks God").

12. Cf. F. S. Spencer, "2 Chronicles 28:5–15 and the Parable of the Good Samaritan,"
WTJ 46 (1984) 317–49.

plied in a completely new direction: The prohibition against bearing false witness is turned *ad personam*: Job is a true witness regarding himself. If he were guilty, he would confess his sin. But he has nothing to confess. He is not concerned with external, social validation, he wants to stand proud in the presence of God and in his own conscience!

Job demands that his listeners write a formal accusation against him. The conceptual context of vv. 35–40 seems to be a court of law. Even if the earth and its soil were called as witnesses—as they once were against Cain—Job would have nothing to fear. On his land, he has done nothing evil, has not cheated, nor ever killed anyone. The idea that the earth (as also the heavens) can act as witness[13] point us to an important tradition-historical context for the verse. This has often been overlooked in recent research, in which the verses are often seen as a displaced claim of innocence[14] and consequently moved in front of v. 35 or removed as an aberrant redactional gloss. The נפש mentioned in v. 39 is most likely to be read as the נפש of God, who is described as the aggrieved owner of the land. This meaning is not very common in the Old Testament but quite possible (see Lev 26:11, 30; Judg 10:16; 1 Sam 2:35; Isa 1:14, 42:1; Jer 9:8, 12:7, 14:19, 15:1, 32:41; Prov 6:16). Yahweh as the "lord and owner" of the land is a common concept.[15] The verse thus seems to indicate that Job is willing to harvest thorns and stinking weeds instead of wheat and barley, if the earth were to witness against him or if God's נפש had been saddened because he had "used the fruits of the field in vain." Nonetheless, neither must he fear this curse.

The phrase "The words of Job are ended" is most often seen as a redactional supplement indicating the end of the words of Job (see also Ps 72:20; Jer 51:64). The phrase may, however, also refer to Job's integrity that was described repeatedly as תם (1:1, 8; 2:3, 9; 9:21; 27:5; 31:6). We may thus translate: "Job's words are without blemish!'" But this remains a mere suggestion.[16]

---

13. M. Delcor, "Les attaches littéraires, l'origine et signification de l'expression biblique 'prendre à temoin le ciel et la terre,'" *VT* 16 (1966) 8–25, refers to the powers of vengeance that guard treaties; see also prophetic judgments as a background for this verse (see Deut 31:28; Ps 50:4; Isa 1:2; Mic 6:2).

14. Job did not exploit the earth he was farming; see G. Fohrer, *Buch Hiob*, 441–42.

15. See J. G. Plöger, "אדמה" *ThWAT* 1:103–4.

16. A. Weiser's interpretation (*Das Buch Hiob* [4th ed.; ATD 13; Göttingen: Vandenhoeck & Ruprecht, 1963] 216) seems quite unlikely. He suggests that Job is "finished": "der hier von ihm eingeschlagene Weg führt nicht mehr weiter" [the way he has pursued does not go any further]; Weiser turns the self-assured declaration into a humble resignation and thus devalues the following theophany and divine speech.

Following this short overview of the chapters, let us summarize the
picture of Job's moral life it portrays:

1. Job values the dignity of women; he protects his family and his
   wife through his moderation and fidelity.
2. He respects the rights of socially inferior groups.
3. He pays special care to the plight of the *personae miserae*—the
   widows, the orphans, the beggars—and actively comes to their
   aid.
4. He resists serving mammon or any other false gods.
5. He even respects the rights of the enemies who hate him and the
   strangers who enjoy his generous hospitality.
6. In his moral courage his despises hypocrisy and false pretense.

The tone of this chapter intends to convince its readers to embrace the
ideal of a moderate, cooperative, generous and charitable, god-fearing,
and self-assured individual. The chapter thus sketches the universal image
of an ideal person.

The intentional omission of the divine Name YHWH (see v. 39 in my
interpretation) also indicates that this ideal is not just limited to an intra-
Israelite context. Here we find an explicit confirmation of what God had
said to the *satan* in the prologue:

> Have you considered my servant Job? There is no one like him on
> the earth, a blameless and upright man who fears God and turns
> away from evil. (Job 1:8)

Like a magnifying glass, the text focuses a whole host of ethical insights
from the Torah, the prophets, the psalms, and wisdom literature.[17]

---

17. E. Osswald, "Hiob 31 im Rahmen der alttestamentlichen Ethik," *Theologische Versuche* 2 (1970) 9–26; G. Fohrer, "The Righteous Man in Job 31," in *Studien zum Buche Hiob* (2nd ed.; ed. G. Fohrer; BZAW 159; Berlin: de Gruyter, 1983) 78–93, disagrees with the character of the text as summary; he suggests reading the entire chapter in the context of wisdom literature and points to the wisdom language and topics throughout the chapter. Fohrer is indeed correct in his concordant list of connections between Job 31 and wisdom literature. Nevertheless, his focus seems quite reductionist. He evidently intends to downplay any connections to prophetic literature, the psalms, or the Torah, which have also been clearly shown in the work of E. Osswald. Fohrer intends to defend his thesis that Job 31 described the final failure of wisdom: "It is an attack on God's own demands, the purpose of which is to show that God is guilty and that in the end man is right." Here we supposedly encounter "man's original sin (namely, he wanted to be God)." "His ethically perfect behavior would lead him into the worst kind of sin" (ibid., 93). If Job 31 would embody the climax of all Old Testament ethics, Fohrer would find himself in the embarrassing position of having to reject Old Testament ethics as a whole. The *imitatio dei*, however, is not a sin, but a basic principle of Old Testament ethics. This has been clearly pointed out in H. van Oyen, *Ethik*

2. Job 31 and the Decalogue

Job's final speech is understood even more clearly when it is compared to the Decalogue. At first glance, it does not appear that this text has much in common with the Ten Commandments. Most research on Job merely indicates in general terms that Job 31 moves a step beyond the ethics of the Ten Commandments.[18] Despite this high praise, this chapter plays a very marginal role in investigations into Old Testament ethics.[19] The morals described in this chapter are sometimes even seen as an elitist morality of especially pious individuals, whereas the Decalogue is seen as "ethics for everyone." Radical positions even describe chapter 31 as sinful hypocrisy.[20]

With 12, the number of Job's virtues does not exactly match the Decalogue. We should also be careful about reducing this number to ten by

---

des Alten Testaments (Geschichte der Ethik 2; Gütersloh: Gütersloher Verlaghaus, 1967), 45, or J. Barton, "Understanding Old Testaments Ethics," *JSOT* 9 (1978) 44–64 (here 60–61).

18. B. Duhm, *Das Buch Hiob* (KHC 16; Tübingen: Mohr, 1897), 145; he writes (ibid., 149): "The chapter represents the high point of Old Testament ethics. The poet not only goes far beyond what a pamphlet could offer in this context. . . , but it also offers something more and higher than the Decalogue and the same as the prophets. . . . Our catechism, if it needed to take something from the Old Testament, should rather have taken this chapter than the Decalogue for the basic tenets of ethics." Such wide-ranging elegies tend to overlook several limitations of the text: Osswald, "Hiob 31," 5, 9, points to critical observations on vestiges of earlier ethics, such as the punishment of the wife for transgressions of the husband (v. 10), eudemonism, and utilitarianism that advocate the good only because it is profitable and avoids punishment (vv. 1–4,21–23). Both extremes must be treated with caution.

19. A few examples include W. Eichrodt, *Gott und Mensch*, vol. 3 of *Theologie des Alten Testaments* (4th ed.; Stuttgart: Klotz, 1961) §22: "Die Auswirkungen der Frömmigkeit im Handeln (Alttestamentliche Sittlichkeit)," 218–63: Job 31 is only mentioned in a footnote (234 n. 90) within a long list; in J. L'Hour, *Ethik der Bundestradition im Alten Testament* (SBS 14; Stuttgart, Katholisches Bibelwerk, 1967): the chapter is not mentioned at all; the same is true for E. Würthwein, *Verantwortung* (Biblische Konfrontationen; Stuttgart: Kohlhammer, 1983). In H. D. Preuss, *Israels Weg mit JHWH*, vol. 2 of *Theologie des Alten Testaments* (Stuttgart: Kohlhammer, 1992), it is mentioned at least five times, including references to the two most important articles on the issue (ibid., 223 n. 179). The chapter itself, however, is not valued highly ("in this 'reflection of male confession' . . . there is much that can be recognized as custom of that time and that Job in a good and just manner not only thought about himself but also felt himself to be connected to and obligated to the community in which he lived" ["da läßt sich in diesem ‚Männerbeichtspiegel' . . . vieles von dem erkennen, was damals Sitte war und von Hiob als einem guten und rechten Weisen, der keineswegs nur an sich dachte, sondern der Gemeinschaft sich verbunden und verpflichtet fühlte, gelebt wurde"; ibid., 223]. We are faced with a completely different situation in E. Otto, *Theologische Ethik des Alten Testaments* (Theologische Wissenschaft 3/2; Stuttgart: Kohlhammer, 1994) 168–71, who presents a detailed analysis of the chapter. Otto, however, limits his discussion to juridicial comments and thus overlooks several important aspects of the text.

20. G. Fohrer, "The Righteous Man in Job 31," in *Studien zum Buche Hiob* (2nd ed.; ed. G. Fohrer; BZAW 159; Berlin: de Gruyter, 1983) 78–93, here 93, reaches the devastating conclusion that Job has fallen into titanic hubris and thus committed the most fundamental sin against God.

emending the text.[21] Even if the chapter is not an original unit, as its irregularities seem to indicate, those who created the final text followed a specific intention. A statistical comparison of the language to that of the Decalogue does not result in any significant terminological connections between the two texts. Neither is the order of the sins (respectively, their opposite virtues) the same. An exception may be seen in vv. 24–32, which does mirror the order of commandments 1 to 4.

Terminological statistics, however, cannot be the only criteria when comparing these texts. The clear differences in form (legal statement versus oath of cleansing) and semantic shape (short legal clauses versus lengthy poetic declarations) necessitate a wider methodological approach.

As demonstrated above, the chapter is structured as a sequence of 12 passages (it is not really appropriate to speak of stanzas), which each refer to a possible sin that Job did *not* commit (vv. 1–34). The sequence does not show an obvious logical order. It appears something like a loose additive collection of ethical statements on central issues. Theological explanations and evaluations are mentioned at irregular intervals; the same is true of potential punishments. The list is concluded with a challenge against God, phrased entirely in juridical language:[22] God is called to stand up as prosecutor and call on the *earth* as his crown witness (vv. 35–40).

If we examine the relationship between these sins (which Job did not commit) and the individual commands in the Decalogue (although printing a comparison of the Decalogue and Job 31 with the appropriate arrows showing similarities is not possible here, it might be of interest for the reader to prepare this type of synopsis for themselves), we notice that there is a subtle and artistic connection between the two. Certain observations will be plausible at first sight,[23] and other connections will be indirect and seem somewhat daring and in need of discussion.

1. The sequence of the Decalogue is reversed in Job 31. "You shall not covet your neighbor's wife" (Deut 5:21) now stands at the beginning and is further emphasized by the repetition in vv. 9–12 (see also vv. 5–8). *The focus of Job 31 is definitely on the second tablet,* on those laws that concern the relationships among humans. The relationship between God and

21. Because vv. 1–3 are missing in LXX*, vv. 1–4 and vv. 38–40 are often seen as being displaced, and we quickly end up with a list of 10 statements; see Fohrer, "The Righteous Man in Job 31," 82–83; idem, *Buch Hiob,* 428. These approaches are to be treated with caution. LXX* may be an intentional emendation of the text and vv. 38–40 are probably an invocation of the earth as a witness.

22. Cf. on this M. B. Dick, "The Legal Metaphor in Job 31," *CBQ* 41 (1979) 37–50; idem, "Job 31, the Oath of Innocence, and the Sage," *ZAW* 95 (1983) 31–53.

23. Cf. the closest would still be שׁוא in Job 31:5/Deut 5:11, 20; more generally עבדי ואמתי (Job 31:13/Deut 5:14, 21) and גר (Job 31:32/Deut 5:14).

human beings only comes into focus in vv. 24–40; even here, the cultic aspects remain marginal. The foundational laws are interpreted through the lens of universal human ethics!

2. Job 31 not only considers the *actual deed*, but also the *basic attitude*. The clearest examples of this internalization of ethical criteria are:

(a) Verse 1 expands the prohibition against coveting the neighbor's wife to all women in general. The text does not state that the "young woman" is married, even though this is assumed by many interpreters. Here we find an intensification of the tendency in the Decalogue to look at the "intent of the heart."

(b) Verse 30 expands the prohibition against taking a name in vain to include the desire for the death of the enemy and any curses intended to accomplish this. The third commandment hardly carries the thought this far. Job 31 thus shows a tendency to *expand* the commandments.

(c) In v. 33, we can see how the perspective moves toward introspection. The text refers to the false witness against oneself in a public setting. This *introspection* is a further *radicalization* of the commandments.

(d) In comparison to the Decalogue, Job 31 contains material that has no parallel in the Ten Commandments. The closest parallel may be the social justification for the commandment to honor the Sabbath in Deut 5:14. This additional material refers to the *sphere of social justice*, which holds a central place in the book of Job. The book does not focus on what wrong was avoided (not having treated the weak with contempt, not having cheated him); it emphasizes what the righteous must do right. They must provide material aid to the poor and show hospitality toward strangers. In the immediate literary context of the book of Job, these statements refute the accusations brought forward by Eliphaz (22:4–11). This additional material, however, also shows how the concepts behind the Sabbath commandment are applied to *concrete situations*: the rights of servants and maidservants are strengthened, as well as the standing of foreigners and cattle. Job displays wide-reaching care and thus fulfills his duty as a wealthy individual. Once again, the text shows an increased focus on the charitable aspects of ethics, even including love of, or at least respect for, one's enemies. The conscience, cultivated by standards put forth in prophetic and wisdom literature, thus bears fruit. In this context, it is no surprise that Job does not mention refraining from murdering anyone. The idea that he might have done anything as crude as breaking the 6th commandment is beyond the scope of the text.

4. The text also shows a *massive extension of the concept of judgment*. Whereas the Decalogue only mentions appropriate punishment in connection with the prohibition against graven images and the profanation

of God's name—both connected to the very nature and justice of God—
Job 31 mentions God's judgment in almost every verse. In vv. 2–4, it is
mentioned extensively. Verse 6 contains the mythical image of the weight
scale, reminiscent of Egyptian judgment in death. Verses 8 and 10–12 focus on the disastrous consequences of adultery (burning everything down
to its foundations). Verse 14 describes the mighty divine judge who acts
on behalf of the poor. Verses 22–23 paint the drastic picture of tearing
arms out of sockets as well as mentioning the fear of God. Verse 28 refers
to sin that is dragged in front of a judge. Verses 35–40 are replete with
the topic of judgment and culminate in v. 40 in the loss of all harvest and
subsequent famine, a punishment equal to the death penalty.

The entire idea of a limited self-curse is taken from a juridical context:
Job's entire existence stands before a court of law. He will be sentenced if
he is not proved righteous. These metaphors of judgment articulate the
awareness that each individual is directly responsible to God. The concept of
individual responsibility is based on the idea that God sees even into the
secrets of individual existence, that he "counts each of my steps" (v. 4),
and that nothing can be withheld from him. Job assumes the omniscience
of God and believes that his life is like an open book. We should not
criticize this sharpened sense of responsibility as utilitarian or eudemonic,
even if this has often been done—especially in Protestant circles under the
influence of Immanuel Kant!

5. The *theological justification* given for ethical conduct is quite remarkable: v. 15 refers to creation theology, according to which the idea of
one creator leads to the conviction that *all* creatures are equal (Job 38–41
even extends this concept to the world of animals and plants). Verse 18 refers to the care and providence that Job experienced from God ever since
his youth and mentions it as the prime motivation for his own treatment
of the poor.

6. Finally, we notice that *the commandment to honor the Sabbath is
completely missing.* This leads us to the observation that the text contains
no cultic legislation at all. In his introspection, Job does not mention offerings, tithes, pilgrimages, or the like. This may be due to the fact that the
fictional character of Job is not an Israelite (just like his female counterpart
Ruth). As a foreigner, he is not bound to observe many of the cultic obli-
gations. On the other hand, it is remarkable that the one commandment
that mentions solidarity with the weak is not referred to at all. It is also
surprising that the ideal wise individual can even be portrayed without
any cultic connections. Job thus becomes a paradigm for universal human
conduct. In this way, Wellhausen is correct in his portrayal of prophetic
and wisdom traditions when he describes postexilic piety as follows: "Die

Moral und nicht der Kultus ist die Quintessenz des Gesetzes; . . . Job 31 ist besonders interessant durch das, was nicht darin vorkommt."[24]

Job 31 is much more closely connected to the Decalogue than might appear at first glance. We can even make the claim that this chapter belongs to the reception history of the Decalogue. New Testament ethics, especially the Sermon on the Mount, shows similar structures when transforming what "was said to our fathers." In both cases, there is no attempt to abolish the law but instead to *apply it to concrete situations.* Both show an *intensification and focus on the attitudes behind the actions* and replace casuistry with *general principles.* Both *expand and radicalize the law* while emphasizing *the role of judgment* and the responsibility of the individual in the presence of an omniscient God. Both marginalize cultic concerns in favor of ethical demands; both favor theological justification for ethical behavior within the context of creation theology and thankfulness.

The lines of tradition that can be seen between the Decalogue and Job 31 show many structural similarities to the appropriation of the law by Jesus (or rather the community behind Matthew). We can draw the conclusion that the ethics of Jesus and the early church are not an oppositional antithesis to late Old Testament ethics *in toto*; we can point to lines of continuity with the later traditions of Israel. We have no evidence of direct connections between the two communities, but the ethical concepts in these texts show clear structural similarities. In any case, this analogy is of high importance in the context of Jewish-Christian dialogue.

3. Conclusion and Continuing Perspectives

The late periods of Old Testament literature tend to stand at the margins of theological interest. Late Old Testament ethics suffers from a negative image. Compared to the glorious ethics of the prophets, it is often seen as a major step backward because it reduces ethics to frozen legalism, with the internal tendency to regulate life with thousands of more-or-less meaningful stipulations. It is regarded as limited national morality that contains double moral standards—standards that can be divided into brotherly love toward those inside and an "oppressive ethics" toward those outside.[25] It is accused of negativity and narrow-mindedness

---

24. J. Wellhausen, *Israelitische und jüdische Geschichte* (5th ed.; Berlin: G. Reimer, 1904) 216. (Morality and not the cult is the essence of the law . . . Job 31 is especially interesting in regard to what it does not mention.)

25. M. Weber, *Das antike Judentum*, vol. 3 of *Gesammelte Aufsätze zur Religionssoziologie* (Tübingen: Mohr, 1921), was highly influential in this regard. He spoke of a paradoxical influence of a prophetic ethics of internal attitude (pp. 332–33) that led to the creation of a Jewish "Pariavolk" (p. 391). It is defined by a voluntary "Ghetto existence" and a

by only invoking prohibitions but giving no guidance for positive action. Cultic concerns seem to dominate ethical principles; love as a motivating factor is replaced by the promise of reward for good behavior. These are the main characteristics suggested for late Old Testament ethics as they are put forward in a classic text on New Testament theology by Rudolph Bultmann.[26] Bultmann is able to quote many Old Testament scholars of his time to support this position.[27] The ethics of Jesus are then seen to be in opposition to the late period, connecting directly back to the glorious era of the prophets.[28] Job's journey inward gives us a different perspective on the value system of the late Persian era (or as I believe, along with a minority of scholars: the Hellenistic period). We see that much of what is portrayed as *exclusively* Christian is anticipated in this text. Job's ethos deserves our highest respect even *sub specie Christi*.[29]

Job does make one theological mistake, however: from his own high ethical standing, he concludes that he is *entitled* to a certain treatment by God. This conclusion is presumptuous on two levels. For one—this is what Job's friends tried to show—even the best of lives falls short of the radical demands of God's holiness and remains dependent on God's grace. Second, Job's arguments imply that he did not act righteously for the sake of righteousness but only with the silent expectation that he was entitled to some kind of reward. In this manner, his ethical reflection turns into hypocritical sin; it mutates into boastful pride. God reacts to Job's ambitions of demanding his happiness on the basis of what he supposedly deserves with silence and contributes to the counseling of Job with word- less judgment.

---

strict dualism between inside and outside ethics (ibid., 4–5). E. Otto, "Forschungsgeschichte der Entwürfe einer Ethik im Alten Testament," *VF* 36 (1991) 3–37, has clearly described these influences. See also the essays on "liberal exegesis" (ibid., 12–14) and "theology" by W. Eichrodt (*Gott und Mensch*, 16–17).

26. R. Bultmann, *Theologie des Neuen Testaments* (6th ed.; Tübingen: Mohr, 1968) 10–21.

27. E.g., I. Benzinger, *Wie wurden die Juden das Volk des Gesetzes?* (Religionsgeschicht- liche Volksbücher für die deutsche christliche Gegenwart 2/15; Tübingen: Mohr, 1908); W. Bousset, *Die Religion des Judentums im späthellenistischen Zeitalter* (3rd. ed.; ed. H. Greß- mann; Tübingen: Mohr, 1926) 119–41.

28. On the so-called "prophetic continuity hypothesis," cf. K. Koch, *Ratlos vor der Apokalyptik?* (Neukirchen-Vluyn: Neukirchener Verlag, 1970) 35.

29. God's evaluation of Job in Job 1:8 and 2:3 confirms this.

CHAPTER 4

Elihu's Last Resort: The Antimonologue

MANFRED OEMING

1. Metaphorical Speech and the God of the Old Testament

In dialectic tension with the many anthropomorphic images of God, the Old Testament simultaneously hesitates to describe God in entirely human terms. God lives "in heaven"; his "throne" is beyond human knowledge; and even the angels cannot grasp him (see Isa 6:1–2). His reality disrupts all categories of human understanding. This is why no graven image may be made of him.[1] Already his "personal name" YHWH is of such sanctity and the fear of abusing this name is so great that it is not pronounced but replaced by a general title.[2] Thus, the Old Testament makes use of a host of *metaphorical* images to describe God's presence in the world indirectly. The most important of these "anti-anthropomorphisms" are: "Name of God," "Glory of God," "Spirit of God," "Word of God," and "Angel of God."[3] The specific power of these theological metaphors lies in their ability to open an imaginative space without setting clear boundaries. This intentional openness when speaking about God reveals and obscures

---

1. "Nothing earthly is able to envision appropriately God, resulting in the paradox that the God of the Old Testament is not invisible, but is also unconceivable" ["Reicht nichts Weltliches aus, Gott zu vergegenwärtigen, so ergibt sich das Paradox, dass der Gott des Alten Testaments zwar nicht unsichtbar, aber auch nicht vorstellbar ist"], W. H. Schmidt, A. Graupner, and H. Delkurt, *Die Zehn Gebote im Rahmen alttestamentlicher Ethik* (EdF 281; Darmstadt: Wissenschaftliche Buchgesellschaft, 1993) 73 (and further literature).

2. This tendency increases throughout the religious history of Israel. Around 250 B.C., the Septuagint displays "a clearly more transcendental conception of God than the Hebrew Bible ["eine deutlich transzendentere Vorstellung von Gott als die hebräische Bibel"], (M. Rösel, "Theo-Logie der griechischen Bibel: Zur Wiedergabe der Gottesaussagen im LXX-Pentateuch," *VT* 48 [1998]) 49–62 (here 59). The paleography of the Qumran texts show that in the first century B.C. the divine name is written in ancient Hebrew script and thus treated differently from the rest of the sacred text.

3. The literature on metaphors in the Old Testament that declare the work of God is very conspicuous; to mention only one: H. D. Preuss, *Theologie des Alten Testaments* (vol. 1; Stuttgart: Kohlhammer, 1991) 183–228.

at the same time. It allows us to *sense something* without *knowing it*. As a *coincidentia oppositorum*, it opens a reality to us that transcends logical bipolarity and can *only* be described in metaphor. The *necessity* of metaphorical speech—transcending the boundaries of what can be said and still give expression to the unspeakable—is a special sign of the logic of theology. An impressive image for this logic is God's revelation to Moses in Exodus 33, where God passes him by, but also covers the eyes of the greatest of all prophets until he is gone.[4] Appropriate theological language remains in the realm of *faith* and does not fall into the illusion of *actually seeing*.

This short introduction is meant to provide the context for the interpretation of the Elihu speeches. The following cannot do justice to the complex argumentation of the six chapters in Job 32–37. Instead, I intend to focus on one image that occurs in Job 33, the מלאך מליץ ('Angel of Intercession'[5]), who will be analyzed *pars pro toto*. I believe it to be the most theologically important text in the Elihu speeches. In the context of the highly debated issue of angelology in the Old Testament, the specific meaning of this text is matter of great controversy.[6]

2. *The Angel of Intercession in Job 33:23*

The most plausible explanation for the literary genesis of the Elihu speeches and their inclusion in the book of Job is greatly debated among

---

4. Cf. M. Oeming, "Gottes Offenbarung 'von hinten': Zu einem wenig beachteten Aspekt des alttestamentlichen Offenbarungsverständnisses," in Gottes Offenbarung in der Welt (ed. F. Krüger; Gütersloh: Gütersloher Verlaghaus, 1998) 292–304.

5. The etymology of לוץ is a matter of debate. How are we to connect the "mockers" in Ps 1:1 and the "translator" in Gen 42:23 with one and the same word? "In the combination of such divergent meanings like 'be insolent/foolish,' 'talk big,' 'scoff,' and 'translate' in a single lemma [*KBL* 3] mirrors the confusion of Hebrew lexicography" ["In der Kombination so weit auseinanderlaufender Bedeutungen wie 'frech/töricht sein', 'groß reden', 'spotten' und 'dolmetschen' unter einem einzigen Lemma (KBL3) spiegelt sich die Verlegenheit der hebr. Lexikographie"]; C. Barth, "לוץ," *ThWAT* 4:567–68. We are forced to determine the meaning of the word *according to its specific context*. In the case of Job 33:22, the situation is especially problematic; we encounter a nameless angel, who stands up personally for an individual whose life is threatened, asking God for forgiveness. We are thus dealing with a kind of "angel of intercession." For more detail, see below.

6. On the issue of מלאך יהוה in an Old Testament / early Jewish context, see W. Bousset and H. Greßmann, *Die Religion des Judentums im späthellenistischen Zeitalter* (HNT 21; Tübingen: Mohr, 1926) 320–31; H. Seebass and K. E. Grözinger, "Engel II–III," *TRE* 9:583–96; M. Mach, *Entwicklungsstadien des jüdischen Engelglaubens in vorrabbinischer Zeit* (TSAJ 34; Tübingen: Mohr, 1992). For a psychoanalytical analysis of angels as the symbol of an aspect of the soul, as a psychic ideal or a phallus symbol, see E. Drewermann, *Tiefenpsychologie und Exegese* (vol. 2; Olten: Walter-Verlag, 1985) 350–51, 558–59; A. A. Bucher, *Bibel-Psychologie: Psychologische Zugänge zu biblischen Texten* (Stuttgart: Kohlhammer, 1992) esp. 40–42.

Old Testament scholars.[7] The same is true for the appropriate theological interpretation of Elihu's five speeches.[8] Some chide him for being a wind-bag or characterize him as a self important know-it-all.[9] In their view, Job does not answer him because he is not worth it.[10] Others recognize in Elihu's speeches the important theological voice of the final redactor of the book of Job. This is where the last and decisive word is spoken, especially in form of a highly developed "pedagogy of suffering."[11] I intend to comment on this long-standing and current debate *following* the exegesis of our text. Everyone agrees, however, that the Elihu speeches repeat what the three older friends had already said or anticipate what God is going to say in his answer to Job. The angel of intercession that will be our focus is found only in the words of Elihu and is a unique aspect of his speeches.

In the second of his five speeches,[12] Elihu, a young and self-confident theologian, challenges Job to an intellectual competition on who had acquired more wisdom (Job 33:1–7).[13] To this end, he first presents a list of

7. See the research summary in H.-M. Wahl, *Der gerechte Schöpfer: Eine redaktions- und theologiegeschichtliche Untersuchung der Elihureden—Hiob 32–37* (BZAW 207; Berlin: de Gruyter, 1993) esp. 8–23. He lists representatives of literary unity as well as the majority position that assumes a complex process of textual growth. I, too, believe that the final form of the speeches is not the result of one hand. S. Lauber, *Weisheit im Widerspruch: Studien zu den Elihu-Reden Ijob 32–37* (BZAW 454; Berlin: de Gruyter 2013) gives a more detailed summary and a new proposal: the Elihu speeches represent a collection of ancient comments on the book of Job by many different students; they found their way from school discussions into the book by an accident—a scribe included the originally independent statements that were be intended for publication. The book of Job is the only biblical book that now includes its own commentary.

8. See the list in Wahl, *Der gerechte Schöpfer,* 23–30.

9. See B. Duhm, *Das Buch Hiob* (KHC 16; Freiburg: Herders, 1897) who sees throughout the Elihu speeches the "inability to understand poets" (ibid., 156 ["Unfähigkeit, den Dichter zu verstehen"]; and its "childlike vanity" ["kindliche Eitelkeit"] attesting to an immature theology (ibid., xi), However, even the *Testament of Job* from the period of the New Testament interprets Elihu as a "son of darkness" guided by Satan (43:5–6), cf. H.-M. Wahl, "Elihu, Frevler oder Frommer? Die Auslegung des Hiobbuches (Hi 32–37) durch ein Pseudepigraphon (TestHi 41–43)," *JSJ* 25 (1994) 1–17.

10. See H. Viviers, "Elihu (Job 32–37), Garrulous but Poor Rhetor? Why is he Ignored?" in *The Rhetorical Analysis of Scripture* (ed. S. E. Porter and T. H. Olbricht; JSNTSup 146; Sheffield: Sheffield Academic Press, 1997) 137–53, who sees Elihu as an anti-model to Job. His verbose statements are *supposed to* stand in comic contrast to the emptiness of content and complete ineffectiveness.

11. In addition to Wahl, *Der gerechte Schöpfer,* see T. Mende, *Durch Leiden zur Vollendung: Die Elihureden im Buch Ijob* (TThSt 49; Trier: Paulinus, 1991).

12. Wahl distinguishes between 1. "Elihu's apologetic self-introduction" (32:6–22); 2. the "speech of the self-manifesting God" (33:1–33); 3. the "speech of the justly avenging God" (34:1–37); 4. the "speech of the inaccessible God" (35:1–16); 5. the "concluding speech of the wonderful-just creator" (36:1–37, 24).

13. Cf. the analysis in Wahl, *Der gerechte Schöpfer,* 53–72; he discerns six (irregular in length) strophes (vv.1–7, 8–12, 13–18, 19–22, 23–28, 29–33). The intent of all God's parlance is the "return of humans" (53).

characteristic quotes taken from Job's speeches that summarize the main aspects of Job's arguments:

> Surely, you have spoken in my hearing, and I have heard the
> sound of your words.
> You say, "I am clean, without transgression; I am pure, and there
> is no iniquity in me.[14]
> Look, he finds occasions against me,[15] he counts me as his
> enemy;[16]
> he puts my feet in the stocks, and watches all my paths."[17]
>
> (33:8–11)

Subsequently, Elihu undertakes the task of refuting Job's claim that God is unjust. It is remarkable, however, that Elihu does not represent Job's position correctly; there is a clear shift in accent: based on Elihu's portrayal, Job's accusation should have been: "God remains silent." Job did in fact voice this accusation—see 30:20: "I cry to you and you do not answer me; I stand, and you merely look at me." Job's main complaint, however, was different, and thus Elihu's words miss the point of the argument:

> But in this you are not right. I will answer you: God is greater
> than any mortal.
> Why do you contend against him, saying, "He will answer none
> of my words"?
> For God speaks in one way, and in two, though people do not
> perceive it.[18] (33:12–13)

Elihu's first explanation for God's silence is a specific interpretation of experiences while asleep: these are not the subconscious, unresolved drives or conflicts, but *God* speaking to human individuals. Unfortunately, the purpose of this mode of communication remains unclear, because the text (vv. 17–18) is very difficult.

---

14. We frequently encounter this basic statement, in which Job proclaims that he has done nothing to deserve the punishment he suffers (see 9:20–21, 9:35, 10:6–7, 16:1–27, etc.). See especially the large defense mounted in chapter 31, an intensive introspection that shows Job's life to conform to the Torah of God.

15. The accusation that God had invented a fictitious cause against Job is not a quotation but a summary by Elihu.

16. God is presented as Job's enemy in 13:24 and 16:9.

17. Verse 11 in total is a quotation from 13:27.

18. This is an extended form of a "numerical saying" (see Wahl, *Der gerechte Schöpfer*, 60 n. 42): "The two divine manners of speech will be developed extensively in vv. 15–18 (dreams) and 19–28 (diseases) and summarized again in v. 29" ["Die zwei Redeweisen Gottes werden in V.15–18 (Träume) sowie 19–28 (Krankheiten) ausführlich entfaltet und V29 wieder zusammengefaßt"].

In a dream, in a vision of the night, when deep sleep[19] falls on
mortals, while they slumber on their beds,
then he opens their ears, and *seals them with a ribbon/bonds.*[20]
that he may turn them aside from their deeds, and keep them
from pride,[21]
to spare their souls from the Pit, their lives from being ended by
a *projectile.* (33:15–18)

As a second argument, Elihu presents the description of a serious illness.
According to the logic of the entire passage, symptoms of such an illness
should also be understood as "divine speech."

They are also chastened with pain upon their beds, and with
continual strife in their bones,
and HE makes them loathe food, and their appetites dainty food.
Their flesh is so wasted away that it cannot be seen; and their
bones, once invisible, now stick out.
Their souls draw near the Pit, and their lives to the angels of
death.[22] (33:19–22)

Even if illness is interpreted in many different ways in the Old Testament,[23]
the most common interpretation understands sickness as a form of punishment that contains an implicit call to repentance and remorse. It is
thus quite tempting to interpret Job's massive physical pain as a divinely
instituted didactic measure. This "pedagogy of suffering" aims to push
an individual to his or her physical limitations, described here as the very

---

19. See M. Oeming, "תַּרְדֵּמָה/רָדַם—schlafen/Tiefschlaf," *ThWAT* 7:358–61.

20. The verse is often vocalized in a different manner: יַחְתֹּם (= 'he seals') is read with
LXX as יָחֵת = 'he scares them'; וּבְמֹסָרָם (= 'with their ribbon') is read as וּבְמֹרָם (= 'with
their admonition'). The interpretation of this term in LXX is remarkable = ἐν εἴδεσιν φόβου
(= 'with images of fear'), see H. M. Orlinsky, "Studies in the Septuagint of the Book of
Job," *HUCA* 33 (1962) 119–51, here 148. We might question the validity of these changes
because they are a considerably simplification of the text in comparison to MT. N. H. Tur-
Sinai, *The Book of Job* (2nd ed.; Jerusalem: Kiryath Sepher 1981) 469 interprets the statement
on the basis of a traditional Jewish evening prayer: ". . .that human eyes may be sealed with
ribbons of sleep."

21. The basic meaning of כסה is 'cover/cover up'; the verb can also refer to sins: see
Ps 85:3, in which God is praised for covering up all the sins of the people; a negative use is
found in Neh 3:37: "Do not cover their sins!"

22. The conjecture mentioned in BHS (= to death) is not necessary. As the Akkadian
musmituti (= 'bringers of death') shows, we can reckon with a vibrant belief in spirits of death
who accompanied the process of dying (see 2 Sam 24:16; 1 Chr 21:15; Ps 78:49).

23. See the overview in M. Oeming, "'Ich bin durchbohrt in meinem Innern':
Krankheit und Leid in der Sicht des Alten Testaments," in *Krankheit und Leid in der Sicht
der Religionen* (ed. M. Oeming; Osnabrücker Hochschulschriften 13; Osnabrück: Univ.,
Fachbereich Erziehungs- und Kulturwissenschaft, 1994) 5–28.

loathing of food. This complete disgust with life is intended to lead the suffering individual to repentance. But is this interpretation justified by the text? Some find an analogy in Job 5:17 where Eliphaz presents his pedagogy of suffering:

> How happy is the one whom God reproves; therefore do not despise the discipline of the Almighty.

I do not believe that Elihu's words in chapter 33 can be narrowed down in this manner. Job 33 describes the cruelty of suffering unto death in all its brutality. Pain is the transition "to the pit." "In lament, the individual senses that he is close to Sheol. He is still merely at the gates at the very boundary, but he is not yet completely surrounded by death. The lamenting individual is standing at the very edge of the abyss."[24] The situation depicted by Elihu is the climax of a drama: All seems lost; the individual can accomplish nothing more on his own. Yet there is no hint of repentance! And then a turning point occurs:

> Then, if there should be for one of them an angel, a mediator,
> one of a thousand, one who declares a person upright,[25]
> and he (the angel? God?) is gracious to that person, and says (to God? to the angel?), "Deliver him from going down into the Pit; I have found a ransom;
> let his flesh become fresh with youth; let him return to the days of his youthful vigor."
> Then he (the angel) prays to God, and he will accept him, he comes into his presence with joy, and God repays him for his righteousness. (33:23–26)

What has happened here? What occasioned this turning point? Why is the person facing death (it is quite unlikely that he has already died[26])

---

24. C. Barth, *Die Errettung vom Tode: Leben und Tod in den Klage- und Dankliedern des Alten Testaments* (ed. B. Janowski; Stuttgart: Kohlhammer, 1997) 91 ["Besonders im Klagelied weiß sich der Einzelne oft lediglich in unmittelbarer Nähe der Scheol. Noch steht er in ihren Toren, also hart an ihren Grenzen; noch scheint er nicht total von ihr umgeben zu sein . . . Der Klagende steht am äußersten Rande des Abgrunds"].

25. יָשְׁרוֹ may refer to God's 'ordinances' or even his judgment; but it could also refer to a person and his rights and duties (see v. 27). The expression seems to oscillate between the two.

26. According to T. Mende, *Das Buch Ijob* (vol. 2; Geistliche Schriftlesung 14; Düsseldorf: Patmos 1994) 185, the images in the text assume that the suffering individual had already died: "Elihu's words about the soul leaving behind the Pit into the the light of the living . . . [is] not only to be understood figuratively, but assumes that the person had truly experienced death" ["Die Rede Elihus vom Zurückkehrenlassen der Seele aus der Grube ins

suddenly brought back into life? The correct understanding of this text is debated.

It should be clear, however, who the suddenly appearing mediator is: it is a nameless angel, one of the myriads of heavenly beings. Older suggestions[27] that identify this mediator as a person (such as a teacher, a prophet, a priest, or a friend) or as the conscience of the sick individual, or even as Christ, are no longer discussed seriously. It is also unlikely that the mediator refers to Elihu himself.[28] What kind of angel is the text talking about and what is his role in the drama? Scholars have proposed the following theories:

1. The text may refer to an *angel of translation* (see Gen 42:23), who translates the hidden language of God for the sinner and explains the correct course of action,[29] thus leading the sinner to repentance. The ransom accepted by God is the repentance offered by the sinner: "The response accepted by God is the remorse of the sinner. *The sinner has paid the ransom himself.* With the help of the *translator,* the *angelus interpres,* the afflicted individual has understood the signs sent by God—his dreams and his suffering—and has paid the necessary price. . . . This is the very *novum* in comparison to the priestly theology of sacrifice."[30] Among those who support this position are G. Fohrer, A. de Wilde, and B. Janowski.[31] Certain

---

Licht der Lebenden . . . [ist] nicht nur bildlich zu verstehen, sondern setzt voraus, dass der Mensch sich wahrhaftig im Tod befunden hat"].

27. Cf., e.g., A. de Wilde, *Das Buch Hiob* (OTS 22; Leiden: Brill, 1981) 316.

28. Cf. A. van Selms, *Job: En praktische Bijbelverklaring* (Kampen: Kok, 1984) 164; A. P. Finnan, *A Rhetorical Critical Analysis of Job 32–37* (Ph.D. diss., The Southern Baptist Theological Seminary, 1988) 173.

29. This is the correct course of action. Influenced by Kant, it has often been understood as "duty").

30. Wahl, *Der gerechte Schöpfer,* 67 (first emphasis mine). ["[Das] von Gott angenommene Lösegeld . . . ist in Form der Bußfertigkeit des Sünders erbracht. *Der reuige Mensch hat es selber gezahlt,* der Heimgesuchte hat die von Gott gesandten Zeichen—die Träume und das Leid—durch den *Dolmetscher,* den *angelus interpres,* verstehen und die zur Umkehr befreiende Buße leisten können. . . : das ist das Eigentliche und das Novum gegenüber der priesterlichen Opfertheologie."]

31. G. Fohrer, *Das Buch Hiob* (KAT 16; Gütersloh: Gütersloher Verlaghaus, 1963) 458–60 (here 460): "The ransom offered by the angel in this context can only constitute the repentance of the sinner who determines to do his duties" ["Das von dem Engel dargebotene Lösegeld kann nach dem Zusammenhang nur die Umkehr des Sünders bilden, der seine Pflichten zu tun sich entschlossen hat"].

De Wilde, *Das Buch Hiob,* 316–17 the ransom here is "certainly the remorse, the repentence, and the vow of the sick one" ["wohl die Reue, die Umkehr und das Gelübde des Kranken"].

B. Janowski, *Sühne als Heilsgeschehen* (WMANT 55; Neukirchen-Vluyn: Neukirchener Verlag, 1982) 149–50: "With regard to the 'ransom' for the sick provided by the advocating angel, the receiver of which according to the context of Job 33:19–30 is God, concerns neither the sickness or the suffering (that God reckons as כֹּפֶר), nor a sin offering for the sick

semantic aspects of the text, however, call this understanding of the angel as a "hermeneutic" catalyst for repentance and teacher of proper remorse into question: "I have found a ransom" (מָצָאתִי כֹפֶר). Do not the semantics of "*to find*" imply that something is already there that can be found? The basic meaning of the term is "to find a specific object whose whereabouts is unknown."[32] It is not possible to "find" preemptive forgiveness that exists only based on the hope of future repentance.

2. Other scholars believe that the angel is an angel of intercession, similar to prophetic intercession. The angel would stand before God and plead the case of the mortally ill individual. I believe that the disagreement, indicated by the bracketed variants in the translation, over whether v. 24 is the intercession of the angel or already a word of God can be decided on the basis of v. 26a, which contains the prayer of the angel, who must therefore be seen as an advocate. An analogy may be seen in the ending of the book of Job, where Job acts as an advocate for his friends (42:8), who are then granted forgiveness by God.[33]

This interpretation also suffers from the fact that it does not do justice to the semantics of *to find something*.[34] If the angel were merely an intercessor, he would utter an intercessory prayer such as: "O God, please show mercy" (compare v. 26) and could not refer to an existing object: "I have found something."

3. The juridical frame of the entire book of Job leads some scholars to interpret these verses within the setting of a legal court.[35] In this view, the angel is a defense lawyer in the court of Yhwh. He takes the side of

---

person, nor even a substitutionary ransom provided by an angelic intercessor, but only about the intercession to enable contrition on the part of the sick person, that is their repentance" ["Bei dem vom Fürsprecherengel bei dem Todkranken gefundenen 'Lösegeld', dessen Empfänger nach dem Kontext von Hi 33,19–30 Gott ist, handelt es sich weder um die Krankheit oder das Leiden (das Gott als כֹפֶר anrechnet) noch um ein Sühnopfer des Kranken noch gar um ein vom angelus intercessor stellvertretend beigebrachtes Lösegeld, sondern allein um das die Intercession ermöglichende Bußverhalten des Kranken, d.h. um dessen Umkehr"]; see Janowski's n. 226 for concurring positions.

32. G. Gerleman, "מצא," *THAT* 1:923. We also find the meanings: 'capture an escapee', 'stand up to an enemy', 'gain a hold over', or in a cognitive sense: 'understand'.

33. Cf., for example, A. Weiser, *Hiob* (3rd ed.; ATD 13; Göttingen: Vandenhoeck & Ruprecht, 1959) 267–68 (on Job 42:8); cf. B. Janowski, "Sündenvergebung 'um Hiobs willen': Fürbitte und Vergebung in 11QtgJob 38,2f und Hi 42,9f LXX," *ZNW* 73 (1982) 251–80; reprinted in idem, *Gottes Gegenwart in Israel: Beiträge zur Theologie des Alten Testaments* (Neukirchen-Vluyn: Nehkirchner Verlag, 1993) 40–69.

34. S. Wagner, "מָצָא," *ThWAT* 4:1043–63 (here 1045), refers to the narrative of Saul who searches for his father's lost donkeys and finds a kingdom and to Abishag of Shunem who is found after searching the entire kingdom. Other objects that are found include a capable wife, wisdom, justice, well-being, the solution to a riddle, and the grace of God.

35. J. Behm, "παράκλητος," *ThWNT* 5:805–11 (here 807–8).

his defendant and pleads for the acquittal of the accused. He lists the basic rights of an individual and insists on fair treatment and then absolves him by paying a "ransom fee."[36] The idea of a heavenly advocate as counterpart to the *satan*[37] stands, however, on shaky semantic ground. In all its breadth of meaning, ליץ never means 'to defend'.

4. Some have supposed in very simple terms that the angel paid the necessary ransom himself.

> The meaning of ransom is not restricted to a payment of money. It may include anything accepted in compensation for an obligation, freeing the indebted party from the obligation. In this case the exact nature of the ransom this angel makes is not specified. Whatever it is, it meets the demands of divine justice and compensates for that person's failures, so that person is freed released the punishment brought on by his errant ways. Once *this angel pays the ransom*, the death angel must leave the offender.[38]

5. How are we to understand the role of the angel? Is he a *translator* of the secret language of God, a "prophetic" *intercessor* or heavenly *advocate*, or is he a generous *sponsor* who pays the "bill" out of his own pocket? Or is he, perhaps, everything at once? I believe that all these interpretations remain very problematic. The text says nothing of oaths or of future accomplishments by the sick individual; instead, it draws our attention to the activity of the angel. The angel does not say: "I will pay for the sin" or "I have found a legal precedent that allows me to pardon him." Instead, he says: "I have found a ransom for his soul."

I would thus like to suggest a new interpretation, which may suffer from the fact that its basic assumption is not mentioned explicitly in the text but can only be seen if we read between the lines. This assumption, however, best allows us to understand the direct meaning of the words. As an explanation of the decisive statement, "I have found a ransom," I suggest we resort to a concept that has been of marginal importance in Christian theology, especially in Protestant circles: the concept of a heavenly treasure of grace. In the context of Job 33, this concept is not to be understood as an egotistical "justification by works" but as an elevated idea of "altruistic reward." According to this idea, the reward for good deeds would benefit not only on those who performed them but could also

---

36. D. N. Freedman and B. E. Willoughby, "מַלְאָךְ," *ThWAT* 4:903.

37. In the background could be the Persian conception of the struggle for the soul between the powers of good and evil (cf. the conclusion of Goethe's *Faust*).

38. J. E. Hartley, *The Book of Job* (2nd ed.; NICOT; Grand Rapids: Eerdmans, 1991) 446 (emphasis mine).

benefit *other* individuals.[39] This complex theological concept has not yet been give proper attention among biblical scholars. Even if its roots reach back to preexilic times, we first encounter it clearly in the Deuteronomistic History. From there it extends into the postexilic period, through the intertestamental period, right up to the New Testament (see Matt 6:21; Mark 10:21 par.; Luke 12:33; 1 Tim 6:19): This concept probably grew out of two similar but separate traditions: First, the idea (originating in the wisdom tradition of a causal connection between action and consequence) that *good works* performed by an individual during his life are not done in vain. They are kept in God's hands[40] and are paid back by him in due time.[41] This idea was amplified early on by assuming that this heavenly treasure of good deeds can also benefit *other* individuals who have no good deeds of their own. The second tradition is the assumption that the *grace* given to an individual by God is so plentiful that it overflows onto other people in his or her vicinity and proves sufficient to forgive their sins as well. These two concepts were combined in DtrH during the Exile. We encounter this combination mostly in reference to David: Israel's sin is to be forgiven "for the sake of David" (בַּעֲבוּר/לְמַעַן). Because of David, the promises to Israel will continue. We encounter similar statements in reference to Abraham

---

39. Cf. K. Koch, "Der Schatz im Himmel" in *Vor der Wende der Zeiten: Beiträge zur apokalyptischen Literatur* (ed. U. Gleßmer and M. Krause; Gesammelte Aufsätze 3; Neukirchen-Vluyn: Neukirchener Verlag, 1996) 267–79. Koch speaks of a "destiny-making sphere of deeds" ["schicksalswirkenden Tatsphäre"]. In his view, the sum of a human life has consequences after death. I believe, however, that Job 33 speaks of a "good" that *benefits others* in this life.

40. D. Zeller, "θησαρός," *EWNT* 2:372–73: "[The notion] ties into the OT view of heavenly storehouses. . . , in which Yahweh stores rain and wind. . . , but also the weapons of his wrath, snow and hail, in order to bring them forth on the day of punishment (Deut 32:34–35; Job 38:22–23; Jer 50:25; Sir 43:14; 1 Enoch 17:3). . . . Intertestamental wisdom spurred on to charity. The money was not lost, but deposited with God and in dire straits brought about blessing (Tob 4:9, 12:8–9; Sir 3:4, 17:22–23, 29:10–12, Pss Sol 9:5). In apocalyptic writings the treasure of good deeds laid up in heaven will first become manifest in the final judgment (1 Enoch 38:2; 4 Ezra 6:5, 7:77, 8:33; 2 Bar 14:12, 24:1; 2 Enoch 50:5)" "[Die Vorstellung] knüpft an die atl. Anschauung von himmlischen Vorratskammern . . . an, in denen Jahwe Regen und Wind. . . , aber auch die Waffen seines Zornes, Schnee und Hagel speichert, um sie am Tage der Strafe hervorzuholen (Dtn 32,34f; Ijob 38,22f; Jer 50,25; Sir 43,14; äthHen 17,3). . . . Die zwischentestamentliche Weisheit spornt zur Wohltätigkeit an. Das Geld sei nicht verloren, sondern bei Gott reponiert und wirke in Notlagen Segen (Tob 4,9; 12,8f; Sir 3,4; 17,22f; 29,10–12; PsSal 9,5). In der Apokalyptik wird der im Himmel zurückgelegte Schatz guter Taten erst im Endgericht offenbar (äthHen 38,2; 4Esr 6,5; 7,77; 8,33; syrApkBar 14,12; 24,1; slavHen 50,5)"]; see C. Begg, "The Access to Heavenly Treasuries: The Traditionsgeschichte of a Motif," *BN* 48 (1985) 15–22.

41. Rabbinic literature refers to this treasure chest of grace as something used to justify the very person who paid into the chest. See the list of rabbinic sources related to Matt 6:19–20 in H. L. Strack and P. Billerbeck, *Kommentar zum Neuen Testament aus Talmud und Midrasch* (4th ed.; Munich: Beck, 1965) 1:429–31.

(Gen 26:24; 2 Kgs 13:23; Sus 3:11; 2 Macc 8:15; Sir 44:24). The clearest passage may be Genesis 18, where Abraham haggles with God over the question whether 50, 40, 30, or fewer righteous individuals are enough to save the cities of Sodom and Gomorrah:

> And the LORD said, "If I find at Sodom fifty righteous in the city, I will forgive the whole place for their sake." . . . Then he said, "Oh do not let the Lord be angry if I speak just once more. Suppose ten are found there." He answered, "For the sake of ten I will not destroy it." (Gen 18:26, 32)

We can hardly assume that Genesis 18 is part of J; rather, it is one of the later texts in the Pentateuch,[42] but it is *part of* the Pentateuch[43] and thus to be dated at least as early as in the 4th century B.C.E. In the Israel of the Hellenistic era, there no doubt existed a theological concept that assumes—not without opposition[44]—the existence of a kind of "heavenly treasure chest of grace" into which the righteous deposit their good deeds and from which "reward" is paid out to less righteous individuals in need of help.[45] The martyr theology of later periods probably gave new impulse to this theory (see 2 Macc 7:9, 23) and caused a shift toward payment only in the life to come: martyrs were comforted by the thought that they would receive their "reward" post mortem. The "treasure of grace" then plays a central role in the New Testament (see Rom 4:25, 5:7–8, 11:28; 1 John 2:12): sins are forgiven "for Christ's sake"; his undeserved death is a "ransom" for our sins.[46]

42. H. Seebass, *Genesis* 2.1: Vätergeschichte 1 (11,27–22,24) (Neukirchen-Vluyn: Neukirchener Verlag, 1997) 134, assumes that the text is a late addition to J and closely related to Ezek 14:12–20.

43. C. Levin, *Der Jahwist* (FRLANT 157; Göttingen: Vandenhoeck & Ruprecht, 1993) 168–70, sees Gen 18:22b–33a as a layered post-redactional supplement in which Abraham becomes the defender of pious Jews.

44. See Ezek 14:12–20, as well as Ezek 18:20, 33:1–16; 2 Kgs 14:6, and Deut 24:16. Each text emphasizes that everyone must pay for their own sin or be rewarded for their own righteousness. These texts categorically reject any notion that extra achievements can be transferred to others.

45. B. Janowski, "Auslösung des verwirkten Lebens: Zur Geschichte und Struktur der biblischen Lösegeldvorstellung," *ZTK* 79 (1982) 25–59; reprinted in *Gottes Gegenwart in Israel: Beiträge zur Theologie des Alten Testaments* (ed. B. Janowski; Neukirchen-Vluyn: Neukirchener Verlag, 1993) 5–39. He examines the legal aspects of ransom in the context of private indemnity, including bribes (Amos 5:12; 1 Sam 12:3; Prov 6:5). His examination culminates in the analysis of Mark 10:45 (and parallels) in combination with traditions from Deutero-Isaiah (especially Isa 43:3–4 and Isa 53).

46. For an interpretation of the violent death of Jesus as an act of salvation, see G. Friedrich, *Die Verkündigung des Todes Jesu im Neuen Testament* (2nd ed.; BTSt 6; Neukirchen-Vluyn: Neukirchener Verlag, 1985); G. Barth, *Der Tod Jesu Christi im Verständnis des Neuen Testaments* (Neukirchen-Vluyn: Neukirchener Verlag, 1992).

We should not mistake this idea with such concepts as those found in
Isa 43:3b or Prov 21:18, where the life of "the nations" is give for Israel
or the life of the "wicked" is given for the righteous as "ransom."[47] Psalm
49:8–9 negates the possibility of ransoming a misspent life entirely.[48]

I would suggest interpreting Job 33:23–24 in the context of the traditions described above. The angel, who comes to the aid of the suffering
individual, would have searched *in heaven* and found a "treasure chest of
grace" that he now offers up for ransom. He offers it to God as payment
for the lost soul (see v. 26a.). The decisive moment in the description of
this text is the encounter between God and the angel: "[Der] entschei-
dende Vorgang der Befreiung vom todbringenden Leid ereignet sich im
himmlischen Bereich zwischen Gott und dem Engel."[49] *God* accepts the
ransom (see Exod 30:12; Ps 49:8–9; Prov 21:18) and subsequently re-
pents from his anger. The repentance shown by the suffering individual is
not the *cause* of God's forgiveness; it is the *result*. The redeemed recognizes God's action and confesses his sins *after the fact.*

> That person sings to others and says, "I sinned, and perverted
> what was right, and it was not paid back to me.
> He has redeemed my soul from going down to the Pit, and my
> life shall see the light." (33:27–28)

Singing is the adequate reaction to God's intervention with and through
the angel; and the lyrics of this song of praise—what a wonderful example
of justification by faith! Despite sin, life was not lost; instead, sin led to the
divine gift of grace.

3. Conclusion:
The Angelus Intercessor
as a Metaphor for God's Saving Action

I believe it to be of utmost importance that we identify the actions
of the angel with the actions of God himself, as is the case in many other

---

47. See D. Vieweger and A. Böckler, "'Ich gebe Ägypten als Lösegeld für dich'": Mk
10,45 as und die jüdische Tradition zu Jes 43,3b.4," *ZAW* 108 (1996) 594–607, who try to
show that this concept is not part of Old Testament traditions and thus cannot be used as a
source for Mark 10:45.

48. See Janowski, "Auslösung des verwirkten Lebens," 32–34; M. Witte, "'Aber Gott
wird meine Seele erlösen'—Tod und Leben nach Psalm XLIX," *VT* 50 (2000) 540–60
(esp. 550).

49. G. Fohrer, *Das Buch Hiob*, 460 (The decisive act of liberation from suffering and
death occurs in the heavenly sphere between God and the angel). Fohrer arrives at this correct conclusion, even if he mistakenly assumes that the remorse of the suffering individual is
the ransom payment.

instances (see Gen 16:7–13; 18:2–10; 22:11–12, 15–18; 31:11–13; Exod 3:2–6; Num 22:35; Judg 2:1–2). The acts of the angel are a visual depiction of the indescribable action of God. God heals, he saves, he punishes, and he proclaims—by means of an angel.

God in Job 33 thus shows mercy on the suffering individual in the form of his angel.[50] This is a typical feature of much biblical language: God allows an intercessory angel, who actually belongs to the sphere of God, to present the good works of the "saints," of the "righteous" (works that he "created" himself by granting faith), and thus wrest forgiveness from him. This is a full-blown description of the saving acts of God: God is reconciled with himself (2 Cor 5:19). The intercessory angel is nothing but a metaphor for this side of the reality of God.

> God indeed does all these things, twice, three times, with mortals,
> to bring back their souls from the Pit, so that they may see the
> light of life. (33:29–30)

The main point of Elihu's second speech is not a highly debatable pedagogy of suffering but rather an unexpected intervention of divine grace (in the shape of an angel) for the salvation of human beings. This interpretation finds its closest support in the work of S. Terrien, who interprets the role of the angel as "one of the thousand messengers of God's judgment and grace."[51] If this interpretation is correct, then Elihu has nothing to fear from a comparison between Job's wisdom and his. The repeated reflection on God's ability to grant grace by means of a heavenly being, even in the face of unredeemable sin, is an important step on the path of suffering.

> Pay heed, Job, listen to me; be silent, and I will speak.
> If you have anything to say, answer me; speak, for I desire to
> justify you.
> If not, listen to me; be silent, and I will teach you wisdom.
> (33:31–33)

---

50. T. Mende, *Das Buch Ijob*, 181.
51. S. Terrien, "Job," in *Interpreters Bible* (ed. L. E. Keck; New York: Abington, 1954) 3:877–1198 (here 1137).

CHAPTER 5

The Encounter with God

MANFRED OEMING

Job has been on a long journey. Through many moving chapters, he has attempted to solve his problem in dialogue with himself and with his friends: "Why is God doing this *to me*? Why do I have to suffer this evil from God?" Job still does not understand what evil he is supposed to have committed. Despite all his friends' thoughts, Job holds on to his innocence (especially in chapter 31)—and to God. He longs for a divine answer before his death; this longing provides the drive for the entire book. Job's last words in 31:35 are:

"This is my longing: That the almighty answers me."

The last wish of the deathly ill Job is a challenge to God.

1. The Structure of the Divine Speeches and Their Main Problems

The text of Yahweh's answer to Job contains a whole host of detailed philological issues that I cannot address in this context[1] because I wish to focus on the main theological aspects of the speeches. The text contains a clear structure: it consists of two parallel sections, each with the following sequence: introductory theophany, divine speech, and Job's answer. The outline below will make this clear. The many questions on the text's literary growth also will not be the subject of discussion here.[2] The fact that

---

1. Cf. P. Ritter-Müller, *Kennst du die Welt? Gottes Antwort an Ijob: Eine sprachwissenschaftliche und exegetische Studie zur ersten Gottesrede Ijob 38 und 39* (Altes Testament und Moderne 5; Münster: LIT, 2000) 20–36.
2. Older literature in H.-P. Müller, *Das Hiobproblem* (3rd ed.; EdF 84; Darmstadt: Wissenschaftlich Buchgesellschaft, 1995), 157–68, und V. Maag, *Hiob* (FRLANT 128; Göttingen: Vandenhoeck & Ruprecht, 1982), 219–26. For more recent voices, see: A. de Wilde, *Das Buch Hiob* (OTS 22; Leiden: Brill 1981); O. Kaiser, *Ideologie und Glaube: Eine Ge-*

the book of Job contains two divine speeches and two answers by Job has led to several different suggestions on whether these are an original part of the book or secondary additions to it.[3] Do we not have to entertain the idea that the text grew continually up to its final form? Also in this regard, I will say very little but would like to limit my remarks to the statement that the text in its final form shows a very clear structure (see below). It is thus plausible that it was composed as a double structure from the beginning, even if smaller sections were added later.

If we follow the course of God's answer, we notice the following: God's speeches are full of a host of "counter-questions."[4] They consist of

fährdung des christlichen Glaubens am alttestamentlichen Beispiel (Stuttgart: Radius, 1984) esp. 92–102; D. O'Connor, "The Futility of Myth-Making in Theodicy: Job 38–41," *PIBA* 9 (1985) 81–99; N. Habel, *The Book of Job* (OTL; London: Cambridge University Press, 1985); H. Rowold, "Yahweh's Challenge to Rival: The Form and Function of the Yahweh-Speech in Job 38–39," *CBQ* 47 (1985) 199–211; D. E. Gowan, "God's Answer to Job: How Is It an Answer?" *HBT* 8 (1986) 85–102; E. Kutsch, "Unschuldsbekenntnis und Gottesbegegnung: Der Zusammenhang zwischen Hiob 31 und 38ff.," in *Kleine Schriften zum Alten Testament* (BZAW 168; Berlin: de Gruyter, 1986) 308–35; S. H. Scholnick, "Poetry in the Courtroom: Job 38–41," in *Directions in Biblical Hebrew Poetry* (ed. E. R. Follis; JSOTSup 40; Sheffield: Sheffield Academic Press, 1987) 185–204; D. W. Jamieson-Drake, "Literary Structure, Genre and Interpretation in Job 38," in *The Listening Heart* (ed. K. G. Hoglund; JSOTSup 58; Sheffield: Sheffield Academic Press, 1987) 217–35; G. Gutiérrez, *Von Gott sprechen in Unrecht und Leid—Ijob* (Fundamentaltheologische Studien 15; Munich: Kaiser, 1988); H.-P. Müller, "Gottes Antwort an Ijob und das Recht religiöser Wahrheit," *BZ* 32 (1988) 210–31; R. Girard, *Hiob: Ein Weg aus der Gewalt* (Zurich: Benziger) 1990 (esp. 178–80); D. Wolfers, "The Lord's Second Speech in the Book of Job," *VT* 40 (1990) 474–99; P. J. Nel, "Cosmos and Chaos: A Reappraisal of the Divine Discourses in the Book of Job," *OTE* 4 (1991) 206–26; F. Gradl, "Ijobs Begegnung mit Gott," in *Ein Gott, eine Offenbarung* (ed. F. V. Reiterer; Würzburg: Echter, 1991) 65–82; T. Schneider, "Hiob 38 und die demotische Weisheit (Papyrus Insinger 24)," *TZ* 47 (1991) 108–24; L. Perdue, *Wisdom in Revolt* (JSOTSup 112; Sheffield: Almond, 1991); G. Fuchs, *Mythos und Hiobdichtung: Aufnahme und Umdeutung altorientalischer Vorstellungen* (Stuttgart: Kohlhammer, 1993) 189–264; J. Lévêque, "L'interprétation des discours de Yhwh (Job 38,1–42,6)," in *The Book of Job* (ed. W. A. M. Beuken; BETL 114; Leuven: Peeters, 1994) 203–22; E. L. Greenstein, "A Forensic Understanding of the Speech from the Whirlwind," in *Texts, Temples, and Traditions* (ed. M. V. Fox, V. A. Hurowitz, and A. Hurvitz; Winona Lake, IN: Eisenbrauns, 1996) 241–58; A. Vonach, "Wer ist es, der den Plan verdunkelt? Die Gottesreden des Ijobbuches als innerbiblisches Paradigma einer Neuentdeckung Gottes durch Entlarvung traditioneller Verschüttungen," in *Gottesentdeckungen* (ed. C. Kanzian and R. Siebenrock; Theologische Trends 8; Thaur: Thaur, 1999) 228–40; M. Köhlmoos, *Das Auge Gottes: Textstrategie im Hiobbuch* (FAT 25; Tübingen: Mohr Siebeck, 1999) 321–25; P. Ritter-Müller, *Kennst du die Welt? Gottes Antwort an Ijob: Eine sprachwissenschaftliche und exegetische Studie zur ersten Gottesrede Ijob 38 und 39* (Altes Testament und Moderne 5; Münster: Lit, 2000). D. J. A. Clines, *Job 38–42* (WBC 18B; Nashville: Nelson, 2011); M. V. Fox, "God's Answer and Job's Response," *Bib* 94 (2013), 1–23.

3. See J. van Oorschot, *Gott als Grenze: Eine Literar- und redaktionsgeschichtliche Studie zu den Gottesreden des Hiobbuches* (BZAW 170; Berlin: de Gruyter 1987).

4. G. von Rad, *Weisheit in Israel* (3rd ed.; Neukirchen-Vluyn: Neukirchener Verlag, 1985) 288.

a chain of rhetorical questions. [5] These questions act as grindstones that pulverize Job. Second, in his questions, Yahweh traverses the barren areas of the world, regions that remain inaccessible for human beings because they are too deep or too high, too mighty or too dangerous. [6] With his questions, Yahweh confronts Job with his own limitations, his weakness, and his impotence. This entails, third, a repeated reference to the world of wild animals that are of no use to human beings, such as the list of ten animals (Job 38:39–39:30) and the description of Behemoth and Leviathan (Job 40:15–41:26). God's care and superior power also extend to these regions outside of the human influence and power. The outline of the divine speeches is shown on p. 71.

Is this complex answer even an *answer*? Job had asked why God allowed him to suffer so greatly. Why *him*? Is this not a sign of indiscriminate use of power? Instead of an answer, Job receives two hours of natural history lessons, a little bit of astronomy, a little meteorology—and tons of zoology, as one scholar sarcastically commented. [7] We would expect something utterly different as an explanation for Job's suffering: information on the wager between God and the *satan*, for instance; or the description of a larger context of human history that might make Job's suffering seem meaningful in the end; or at least a plausible reflection on the purpose of Job's suffering in the course of his own life, as was presented by Elihu is his speeches. [8] Christian readers might expect a statement of God's compassion and his solidarity with Job's suffering. None of this is mentioned. Job's suffering is not explained in terms of its necessity for the course of human history or even Job's own psychological journey. There is no sentimental numbing of suffering as an "earthly delight in God"; no word is mentioned of God's compassion. The mystery of Job's suffering is not resolved. It seems as if God's speech is anything but a response to Job. Instead, God pushes aside all of Job's questions in an arrogant and narcissistic display of superiority. The human world is surprisingly not mentioned *at all*. On the contrary, 38:26 speaks of the desert "where no humans

---

5. The more descriptive passages may be later additions to the text.

6. Compare also Psalm 139, where these remote regions are connected to the presence of God. The gates of the shadows of death were referred to frequently in patristic literature; see R. Gounelle, "Le frémissement des portiers de l'Enfer à la vue du Christ: Jb 38,17b et trois symboles de foi des années 359–360," in *Le Livre de Job chez les Pères* (Cahiers de Biblia Patristica 5; Strasbourg: Center d'Analyse et de Documentation Patristiques, 1996) 177–214.

7. Girard, *Hiob*, 179.

8. Through suffering, God opens the ears of the wicked. See Job 36:10–11 (He opens their ears to instruction, and commands that they return from iniquity. If they listen, and serve him, they complete their days in prosperity, and their years in pleasantness).

First Speech	
I.	Report of a theophany in a storm; God accepts Job's challenge (see 31:35) and answers (38:1–3).
II.	First divine speech: By means of rhetorical questions (who did . . . ? Where were you. . . ? Can you. . . ? Do you know. . . ?) God encircles the outermost boundaries of creation (38:4–21).
	(A) Order and boundaries of the *world below:* the earth since its founding (4–7) the sea in its primal extension (8–11) the rising of the sun as a means against the wicked (12–15) primal sources and gates of death (16–20) ironic interlude: ". . . you know this of course" (21)
	(B) Guidance of the *world above* Origin of weather: snow, hail etc. (22–30) the binding of the stars (31–33) clouds and rain (34–38)
	(C) Gods actions in the realm of the *wild animals* ("Can you give prey to the lioness?" etc.) (38:39–39:30):
	1. lions (38:39–40) food
	2. ravens (41) food
	3. ibex (39:1a) birth
	4. stag (1b–4) birth
	5. wild donkey (5–8) freedom
	6. wild ox (9–12) freedom
	7. ostrich (13–18) carelessness
	8. horse (19–25) fearlessness
	9. falcon (26) inaccessibility
	10. eagle/vulture (27–30) prey and blood[7]
	(D) God's challenge to Job: "Answer!" (40:1–2)
III.	Job's first answer to Yahweh ("I am too insignificant. What should I answer?") (40:3–5).
Second Speech	
I.	Second theophany in the storm (40:6); God answers Job and challenges him to answer him back (7–14).
II.	Second divine speech as a mixture of description of nature and rhetorical questions
	(A) Behemoth (giant hippopotamus) (40:15–24)
	(B) Leviathan (giant crocodile) (40:25–41:26).
III.	Job's second answer (42:1–6) (". . . now my eyes have seen you. I thus withdraw and repent in dust and ashes").

exist, where no man lives." Even the animals mock and laugh at the cities
of men (39:7, 18) and their fortifications (41:21). How did the author of
Job intend these divine speeches to be an *answer*?

2. *Suggestions from the History of Scholarship*

Because the intention of God's speeches is far from obvious, it comes
as no surprise that there are many different proposals on how they should
be interpreted. I would like to distinguish eight different types.

(A) Some scholars believe it is irrelevant *what* Yahweh says. It is only
important *that* Yahweh speaks at all. The encounter with God in itself
lays to rest all questioning and all doubt, not because all open issues are
be clarified but only because there is communion with the living God. It
seems to be a basic principle of dialectic theology *that* God has spoken
and that God as the completely other has revealed himself while simultaneously remaining the boundary of human existence. In his commentary,
Franz Hesse assumes that a theophany originally stood at the end of the
book and that the divine speeches were added later, an unfortunate development in his view.[9]

The vast majority of scholars, however, assume that it is not enough to
point to the fact *that* God spoke. It is also necessary to come to terms with
what God actually said and apply it to the problem of Job. The opinions
on how this is to be done vary greatly.

(B) The divine speeches intend to be a *skeptical answer*; they confront
Job's expectations by *deflating them*. The Jewish exegete Matitiahu Tsevat
states: "Divine justice is not an element of reality. It is a figment existing
only in the misguided philosophy with which you have been inculcated."[10]
The divine speeches are skeptical criticism of pure wisdom that can only
fail to explain life's ultimate mysteries.[11]

(C) The divine speeches *admit* that God is trying to combat chaos
and destruction in the world. He is not, however, powerful enough to accomplish this task. God himself shows weakness when facing the constant
onslaught of evil.[12]

(D) The divine speeches try to *hide* the fact that God himself is evil.
This interpretation was put forward by Ernst Bloch and Carl Gustav Jung.

---

9. F. Hesse, *Hiob* (ZBK 14; Zurich: TVZ, 1978) 11–12.
10. M. Tsevat, "The Meaning of the Book of Job," *HUCA* 37 (1966) 73–106, (here 100).
11. K. J. Dell, *The Book of Job as Skeptical Literature* (BZAW 197; Berlin: de Gruyter, 1991).
12. See Rabbi H. Kushner's well-known book: *When Bad Things Happen to Good People* (New York: Schocken, 1983) 31–42.

Job is put down, intimidated, and silenced by God's boastful reference to the infinite distance between creator and created beings. "Yahweh's speeches pursue the unreflected but obvious goal of demonstrating the brutal superiority of the demiurge. . . . God has no intention of being just, he insights that his power takes precedence over justice" [13] By creating this questionable demonstration of infinite divine superiority, the author is presenting a subtle form of religious criticism by allowing Yahweh to destroy his own honor and glory through his own words.

(E) The divine speeches intend to provide *liberation* from all burning questions. The absence of any answer to the question of why suffering occurs *is the answer*. H. D. Preuss states: "The solution lies in the liberation from the question." [14] Samuel Terrien agrees: "Job is invited in effect to liberate himself from the microcosm of his egocentricity, to borrow the perspective of God without pursuing the mirage of self-deification, and to discover the broad horizons of the macrocosm of life on the grand scale." [15]

(F) The divine speeches intend to *convince* Job of the loving care of God and lead him to the realization that his suffering is also a part of God's loving regimen. He can trust in God even when he does not understand him. [16]

(G) God says nothing new in comparison to the friends. This is especially true for Elihu (Job 36–37). The entire spectacle surrounding the storm is mere dramatic stage setting. The book only intends to be read as *satirical entertainment*. [17]

(H) The divine speeches admonish Job to *imitate God* and fight against injustice. "In his lament, Job holds God accountable without

13. C. G. Jung, *Antwort an Hiob* (Olten: Walter, 1973) 31 and 23. ["Die Reden Jahwes haben den zwar unreflektierten, aber nichtsdestoweniger durchsichtigen Zweck, die brutale Übermacht des Demiurgen dem Menschen vorzuführen. . . . Gott will gar nicht gerecht sein, sondern pocht auf seine Macht, die vor Recht geht."]

14. H. D. Preuss, "Die Frage nach dem Leid des Menschen: ein Versuch biblischer Theologie," in *Altes Testament und christliche Verkündigung* (ed. M. Oeming and A. Graupner; Stuttgart: Kohlhammer, 1987) 52–80 (here 68). ["Die Lösung besteht in der Erlösung von der Fragestellung."]

15. S. Terrien, "The 'Yahweh Speeches' and Job's Response," *RevExp* 68 (1971), 501–2.

16. P. P. Szczygiel, *Das Buch Job* (*HSAT* 5/1; Bonn: Hanstein, 1931) 205: "It is instead that undeserved suffering must also have its motivation in God's love for Job; that is, it no longer is genuine proof of divine wrath and the annulment of divine friendship and being the child of God, but rather a special demonstration of love" ["Vielmehr müssen auch die unverdienten Leiden . . . ihr Motiv in der Liebe Gottes zu Job haben; d.h. sie sind nicht mehr vollgültiger Erweis des göttlichen Zornes und der Aufhebung der Gottesfreundschaft und Gotteskindschaft, sondern ein besonderer Liebesbeweis"].

17. So, e.g., B. Zuckerman, *Job the Silent: A Study in Historical Counterpoint* (New York: Oxford University Press, 1991).

contributing anything to the fight against the very suffering that he be-
moans. He challenges God to become active and is forced to experience
that God is indeed active, but that God's activity must find a counterpart
in human activity."[18]

(I) The final speech teaches the need for *real fidelity in the face of
divine injustice.* "Job and his friends agreed on human wretchedness, but
they were, ironically, wrong. Humans have in their power the ability to
give God something he deeply desires: unbought human loyalty, a stance
of unconditional faith, even in the face of divine injustice. . . . The Theophany shows a God whose care for the world of nature hints at his care
for humans. The reader, unlike Job, knows that Job's suffering is important to God, as establishing the possibility of true human loyalty."[19]

The decisive interpretive landmarks are: (1) Does the content of the
speeches matter, or is the theophany itself what is important? (2) Should
we understand the speeches positively as expressions of God's saving action, or are they negative, a distraction from the weakness of God or even
a frivolous religious criticism of God? (3) Are God's questions cynical or
even callous, or do they intend to inspire consent? No matter how we
answer these questions, the reasons for the selection precisely of animals
remains a mystery.

3. The Motif of the "Lord of the Animals"

It is not surprising that past research has left us with the impression
that scholars tend to read more of their own theological opinions into the
divine speeches than extract meaning from them.[20] Recent insights into
the iconography of the ancient Near East have created a more solid basis
on which to proceed. Othmar Keel has made important contributions to
the iconographical study of the ancient Near East, especially in regard
to interpreting the Psalms, the Song of Songs, and also the book of Job.
Keel's interpretation is founded on the analysis of the specific animals men-

18. J. Kegler, "'Gürte deine Lenden! . . .' Die Gottesreden im Ijob-Buch als Aufforde-
rung zur aktiven Auseinandersetzung mit dem Leid," in *"Dass Gerechtigkeit und Friede sich
küssen (Ps 85, 11)": Gesammelte Aufsätze, Predigten, Rundfunkreden* (ed. J. Kegler; BEATAJ
48; Frankfurt: Lang, 2001) 278–93 (here 291). ["Ijob macht Gott in seinen Klagen verantwortlich, aber er leistet keinen eigenen Beitrag zur Überwindung der Leidstruktur, die er
lauthals beklagt. Er fordert Gott auf, aktiv zu werden, und muss nun erfahren, dass Gott
aktiv ist, aber dass Gottes Aktivität eine Entsprechung in der menschlichen Aktivität haben
muß."]
19. Fox, "God's Answer and Job's Response," 23.
20. This is the accusation in the article by Gowan, "God's Answer to Job: How Is It
an Answer?"

tioned in the divine speeches. Earlier research had seen this list as a more-or-less arbitrary collection of wild and untamable animals. By referring to many examples from the area of glyptic art, Keel is able to show that this list is not random. These specific animals occur over and over again in a specific ancient Near Eastern context—the "Lord of the Animals."

This motif is ambivalent: "The central character in the composition sometimes appears as a tamer, sometimes as a protector, of the animals."[21] This entails a basic problem: can we truly connect various different, even contrary aspects (hunter—protector) to one and the same idea while applying different emphasis to each specific situation? Research on the motif of the "Lord of the Animals" has not yet answered this question satisfactorily[22] and still requires further reflection to determine the precise meaning of the iconographic motif. We can, however, state that the aspects of domination and hunt explain most if not all of the images relevant for the book of Job. In the images in Keel's collection, a deity or a king dominates almost all of the animals mentioned in Job by grabbing their horns, binding, hunting, or killing them. A great many stamp-seal impressions from the Sumerian period right up to the Hellenistic period clearly show how widespread this motif was for more than 2,000 years of ancient Near Eastern history. Regardless of variation in details, we can recognize one basic motif: a deity or a king stands at the center of the image and grabs the various animals by their hind legs or their neck. It is evident that both the animals as well as the hero can have wings; they thus represent more than "natural beings." Very similar compositions occur with different animals. Keel shows that the ten species mentioned in Job (lion, raven, deer, ibex, wild donkey, wild ox, ostrich, horse, falcon, and vulture) occur on these stamp impressions. This is the important connection between glyptic and textual evidence.

In his interpretation of Job, Keel presents images from various time periods and different places. In the following, I will only refer to images

---

21. O. Keel, *Jahwes Entgegnung an Ijob: Eine Deutung von Ijob 38–41 vor dem Hintergrund der zeitgenössischen Bildkunst* (FRLANT 121; Göttingen: Vandenhoeck & Ruprecht, 1978) 86. ["Die zentrale Figur der Komposition erscheint bald mehr als Bändiger, bald mehr als Beschützer."]

22. On this issue, see the short article by P. Calmeyer, "Herr der Tiere/Herrin der Tiere," *RLA* 4:334–35 and especially Keel's own work: O. Keel, *Jahwes Entgegnung* (see n. 21 above), 86–125; Keel and C. Uehlinger, *Göttinnen, Götter und Gottessymbole: Neue Erkenntnisse zur Religionsgeschichte Kanaans und Israels aufgrund bislang unerschlossener ikonographischer Quellen* (QD 134; Freiburg: Herder, 1992). On the Lord of the animals as a female figure, see U. Winter, *Frau und Göttin: Exegetische und ikonographische Studien zum weiblichen Gottesbild im Alten Israel und in dessen Umwelt* (2nd ed.; OBO 53; Freiburg, Switzerland: Universitätsverlag / Göttingen: Vandenhoeck & Ruprecht, 1987; H. Weippert, "Die Kesselwagen Salomos," *ZDPV* 108 (1992/93) 8–41 (here 34–35).

that were found in Palestine itself and date to the time when the book of Job could plausibly have been written—that is, from the 8th century B.C.E. (conservatively speaking) to the Hellenistic era.[23]

An impression of the royal Sargonid stamp-seal, found on a stamped bulla in Samaria, may give a first impression of this motif: a royal figure grabs a lion by his mane and holds him up with his bare left hand . His right hand brings a dagger up to the chest of the beast (fig. 1).[24]

A similar theme is found on Neo-Assyrian cylinder seals. These were probably not of local Palestinian origin but were imported into Palestine (figs. 2–5): A winged(?) genius fights with a sword against an ibex (fig. 2).[25]

A kneeling archer fights against an already submissive(?) ox or gazelle(?) with an unusually long tail(?) (fig. 3).[26]

A figure with strange armament, perhaps a stylized bow(?) or shield(?) and a spear(?) is shown in conflict with two chimeras consisting of lion

23. Together with C. Uehlinger, Keel has made this material wonderfully accessible. See Keel and Uehlinger, *Göttinnen, Götter, Gottessymbole.* Thanks to Herder Verlag for granting permission for the republication of the following images, all of which are taken from the volume by Keel and Uehlinger, with permission.

24. See G. A. Reisner et al., *Harvard Excavations at Samaria* (Cambridge, MA: Harvard University Press, 1924) pl. 56a; printed following Keel and Uehlinger, *Göttinnen, Götter, Gottessymbole,* 325, fig. 278b.

25. Taken from Keel and Uehlinger, *Göttinnen, Götter, Gottessymbole,* 329, 282a; found at Gezer; cf. R. Reich and B. Bradl, "Gezer under Assyrian Rule," *PEQ* 117 (1985), 41–54 (here 46–47).

26. Keel and Uehlinger, *Göttinnen, Götter, Gottessymbole,* 329, 282b; found at Megiddo.

and eagle. The scene remains somewhat unclear. Is the figure taming the animals or fighting against them? Does the placement of his foot on the rear part of the smaller winged griffin signal domination or protection?[27] I believe the symbolism to be one of domination. Ps 8:6 describes the ruling power of human beings with the words: "You have given them dominion over the works of your hands; you have put all things under their feet" (fig. 4).[28]

The last example from this period is the image of a deity who is tightly holding two winged creatures, probably an ox and an ibex. The understanding of this example as battle is not as clear in this case. The image may communicate peaceful rule (fig. 5).[29]

Two Persian images from the 6th century (figs. 6 and 7) show a king who is grabbing a lion-eagle chimera by its neck (the right hand is no longer visible). The second image shows a winged ox held by his horns by the right hand of the king; his left hand brings up a dagger (fig. 6);[30] (fig. 7).[31]

Two examples from the Greek era show very similar characteristics. The first displays Bes as "Lord of the Lion," and the second shows Hercules, who is wearing a lion's skin and skull. He is swinging a club at a

---

27. See 1 Kgs 5:17; Ps 18:39, 47:4; Lam 3:34; these texts speak of placing enemies under the feet—i.e., under the complete control—of the king (less strong in Ps 8:7).
28. Keel and Uehlinger, *Göttinnen, Götter, Gottessymbole*, 329; found at Megiddo.
29. Ibid.; found at Dor.
30. Ibid., 433, fig. 360a; a bulla found at Samaria
31. Ibid., fig. 360b, scaraboid from Tell Keisan.

still living lion that he is holding by its tail. At his side is a hunting dog(?) (fig. 8);[32] (fig. 9).[33]

The last example is a particularly beautiful image originating locally in Palestine (fig. 10).[34]

The image is clearly marked into two halves by the line in the middle. The upper register clearly shows the motif of the "Lord of the goats," which is paralleled by a hunting archer [35] aiming his bow at a gazelle in flight. At the same time, he is holding a winged lion at bay.

Keel offers convincing interpretations of these scenes: the animals are *symbols* of the power of Chaos. They are the representatives of a force of "anti-culture"; they are personifications of everything that threatens human and other life. God, or the king, is depicted as the "Lord of these animals"; he is thus lord also of the forces of chaos with all their blood-lust, wildness, and ferocity. These animals live in remote regions that are inaccessible and of no use to human beings: in thorny brush, in rocky mountains, in the desert, and high up in the air. Yet the "Lord of the animals" controls and dominates them all. The main thrust of these images is to depict the king, the genius, or God as someone who holds these animals at bay (and with them all symbolic-mythical threats to existence), vanquishes them, and even kills them.[36]

It is but a small step from these ancient Near Eastern images to the Old Testament text, where we encounter Yahweh as the "Lord of the animals." According to Keel, the first divine speech, with its list of animals, in-

---

32. Ibid., 437, scaraboid from Atlit.

33. Ibid., same locality.

34. Ibid., 359, fig. 308. Cylinder seal from Beth-Shean, late 8th or early 7th century.

35. I am not convinced by Keel's conclusion that the astral elements stand merely in paratactic sequence without interpreting each other.

36. I would like to emphasize once again that the aspect of protection cannot be seen in these images.

tends to make the following statement: "There is no lack of chaotic forces in the world with impressive ferocity and immense destructive power. But the world in not without plan, without order. Yahweh contains the chaos without reducing it to a boring rigid order."[37] God's reign over this world is a pugnacious rule over forces full of oppositional energy.[38]

In answer to the question of the book of Job, the question of suffering and evil in the world, Keel does not look to Job's guilt (as the friends do), or to God's injustice (as Job does), but to a *third* force introduced, in his opinion, by the divine speeches. This force consists of the powers of chaos, who exist as "evil powers outside of God and mankind" which explain "the relative autonomy that evil has in the world."[39] In this manner, "The divine speeches grant a certain amount of autonomy to the forces of chaos and evil in the world and thus remove responsibility from God, who is no longer responsible for everything and all that happens in the world."[40] Keel draws parallels to the idea of the *satan* in the narrative frame and believes that we can trace the beginnings of a development that reaches further into apocalyptic and New Testament ideas of Satan and his kingdom as opposition to the kingdom of God.[41] In the typology of interpretations listed above, Keel belongs to category C: God is not almighty; he must deal with powerful elements that exist alongside him.

As much as Keel's interpretation is an important step forward and as much as he has found support for his ideas,[42] I do believe that a few problems still remain:

If we take a close look at the images, we see a clear stratification of power. The central figure overpowers and subdues his opponents. Yet in the book of Job, God does not grab the lion by its hind legs, or strangle, stab, or club it. He does not hunt and kill the ibex; he does not grab the

---

37. Keel, *Jahwes Entgegnung*, 125. ["Es fehlt in der Welt nicht an chaotischen Mächten von eindrücklicher Wildheit und gewaltiger zerstörerischer Kraft. Aber die Welt ist doch nicht ohne Plan, ohne Ordnung. Jahwe hält das Chaos im Zaum, ohne es in eine langweilige, starre Ordnung zu verwandeln."]

38. Ibid., 156: "Dominion over a vital, intractable, wild, resistant word" ["Herrschaft über eine vitale, widerspenstige, wild sich wehrende Welt"].

39. Ibid., 157 ["Unheilsmächte außerhalb Gottes und der Menschen"]; [die relative Eigenständigkeit, die das Böse in der Welt besitzt"].

40. Ibid. ["räumen die Gottesreden chaotischen und bösen Mächten in der Welt einen gewissen Platz ein und entbinden so Gott von der direkten Verantwortung für alles und jedes, das in der Welt geschieht"]. This statement is true for both(!) of the divine speeches.

41. Cf. ibid., 158.

42. E.g., J. Ebach, "Hiob," *TRE* 15:369–70; E. J. Waschke, " 'Was ist der Mensch, dass du seiner gedenkst?' Theologische und anthropologische Koordinaten für die Frage nach dem Menschen im Kontext alttestamentlicher Aussagen," *TLZ* 116 (1991) 801–12, (esp. 808–10); G. Fuchs, *Mythos und Hiobdichtung*, 210–11.

ostrich by its neck. Quite the opposite is true. God is the one who feeds
the carrion to the ravens; he is the one who provides the blood that the
vultures drink; he grants freedom to the wild ox. He knows and guaran-
tees the rhythms and orders of all the wild animals. Keel seems to notice
this discrepancy and emphasizes that Yahweh shows his power by the very
fact that he allows them to live freely.[43] Yet we must recognize that the
Old Testament text modifies the ancient Near Eastern motif! Keel tries
to escape this conclusion by pointing to the ambivalence of the motif and
speaking of Yahweh also as a protector, even though this is not justified
by the visual material he presents. We must conclude that the motif of the
"Lord of the animals," with its depiction of domination, hunt, and killing
actually *does not match* the activities described in the divine speeches.[44]
In these texts, God is the good father who protects and cares for these
animals. An equivalent visual program would portray God as a zoo direc-
tor, forest ranger, or game warden.

Once we arrive at this conclusion, God's answer to Job becomes even
more mysterious. In response to his lament that the world is full of suffering, and thus chaotic, God answers: "Yes, you are correct. And I, God,
have created these forces of chaos and I sustain them and care for them.
I am also the God of the wild animals." Does this answer not lead to an
absurd increase in Job's suffering? Why does Yahweh not eliminate these
beings that symbolize all that is life-threatening? Why is he so different
from all other kings and gods in Israel's surroundings?

4. The Two-Fold Purpose of the Divine Speeches

God forces Job to realize that the horizon within which he acts as
creator *is much larger than the horizon of human culture.*[45] The creative
acts of God extend way beyond the human sphere. This becomes clear in
the list of animals in 38:39–39:30 as well as in the cosmology of the first
speech (38:4–38). God leads Job through the underworld, the uninhab-
ited desert, and the region of the stars and weather. The third speech,
finally, deals with Behemoth and Leviathan. Job is told that God made Behemoth, "just as I made you" (40:15), and that God plays with Leviathan

---

43. "[Yahweh is lord] especially in that it is he who grants them their freedom"
["[Jahwe ist Herr] gerade dadurch, dass er es ist, der sie in ihre Ungebundenheit entlässt"];
Keel, *Jahwes Entgegnung.* 83.

44. For a similar argument, see U. Neumann-Gorsolke, *Wer ist der "Herr der Tiere"?
Eine hermeneutische Problemanzeige* (Biblisch-Theologische Studien 85; Neukirchen-Vluyn:
Neukirchener Verlag, 2012).

45. The theological logic of the divine speech is much closer to Ps 139 than to Ps 8
or Ps 104.

(40:29). God thus operates in a world that is also occupied by gigantic forces alien and dangerous to human life. God is the lord over *all* spheres of creation. Job probably never dreamed of the fact that God also cares for the creatures that symbolize chaos. There is no dualism consisting of God and (human) culture on the one hand and animals and chaos on the other. The first commandment is applied radically to everything: God is lord over everything. He also gives prey to the predator and vitality and freedom to the wild ox. He even cares for the ostrich, of which the text states that it had lost its wisdom and no longer cares for its offspring (39:16–17). There is no *anthropocentrism*[46] with God; instead, Job (and the readers) must painfully extend their own horizon. The forces of chaos—symbolized by these undomesticated, dangerous, and life-threatening animals—they, too, are part of God's cosmos according to his will. It is God's will, even if it causes suffering for human beings.

How does this explain why Job had to suffer? Job had asked: "What did I do to deserve this?" God does not answer this question, and this is the second purpose of the divine speech. This silence can hardly be understood as bitter irony.[47] In the intention of the author of Job, the speeches point to a larger order that surrounds human life. The world is not chaotic as Job had implied (Job 9; 16:12–14). On the contrary, God has given proper place to the sea, and he has set the boundaries of the stars. God sustains the wild animals; he "steers" Behemoth and Leviathan. *This* cosmos replaces Job's own narrow cosmos. By not answering Job's question and justifying his actions, God transforms both the questioner and his question. In his question, Job had created a frame into which he had pressed God; he had tried to force God onto a "Procrustean bed" of his own ideas of a "just order."

What remains, however, is the question of the meaning of suffering. It remains open, at least from an anthropocentric point of view. Instead, the text describes God's care for wild animals that are of no use to humans and that dwell in inaccessible regions of creation. All this is harsh mortification. God expects Job to accept this hard truth; he painfully wipes away Job's own fantasies of his own importance. Can we accept that a suffering

---

46. As can be seen in his later publications, Keel has come very close to this line of interpretation without accepting the lack of coherence to his former position. See idem, "Antropozentrik? Die Stellung des Menschen in der Bibel," *Orientierung* 51 (1987) 221–33; see also C. Uehlinger, "Vom Dominium terrae zu einem Ethos der Selbstbeschränkung? Alttestamentliche Einsprüche gegen einen tyrannischen Umgang mit der Schöpfung," *BL* 64 (1991) 59–74 (esp. 66–67).

47. See Ritter-Müller, *Kennst du die Welt?* 263–78, and the citation ibid., 277, on the idea that God uses irony as a didactic means of transforming Job's incorrect worldview and faulty view of God's action in the world.

individual is given such an answer? From a perspective of pastoral care, can we stop here and let suffering remain incomprehensible? Is it enough to realize that we are only part of a larger order of things? Maybe there is more truth to this than we would like to believe. Perhaps this mortification is necessary and healthy. Individuals who question the proper function of God's order, who demand justice from God, are given the sobering answer: "Who are you? Where were you? What do you really know?" This is not a brutal put down. It is the neutral placement of human beings in the larger scheme of things, a placement that is far below God, a place among all other creatures that are also important to God. Individual human beings are not the center of God's universe. Humans are below God in a creation that also includes forces of chaos. Beyond the horizon of humans, God has created powers that he sustains and cares for. This is a great rebuke and disappointment.

Nonetheless, the answer to Job also contains an element of good news. Connected to the disillusionment is a promise of grace. In this, model (A), which emphasizes the importance of the theophany itself, is given its due: "And God answered Job." Job needed to learn the sobering truth: "Who do you think you are? What do you really understand? What do you presume for yourself?" — but Job *did receive an answer*. What God says diminishes human importance and places him within the greater context of creation. The fact, however, that God speaks to Job elevates him and grants him a place of special dignity. God does not put Job off; he confronts him with a harsh correction of his position. Job's entire egocentric, anthropocentric system is demolished; his own importance is put in its place. Once Job learns that God does not remain hidden despite all the mysteries of the world, once he encounters him in his word as the living and sovereign ruler, once he allows himself to be chastened, Job's anger subsides and his accusation against God falls silent. On the basis of his encounter with God,[48] Job is empowered to accept his suffering anew. The problem of suffering has not been solved, neither on a practical nor a theoretical level. The meaning of suffering has not been articulated clearly, and the world still remains full of pain. But God has granted Job dignity by appearing to him in the storm and allowing him to hear his word. In this manner, he elevates Job above all other creatures and grants him a special place in this world. This is the gospel that is contained in the midst of the harsh disappointment.

---

48. On the central importance of the category of "encounter," see O. Fuchs, *Klage als Gebet: Eine theologische Besinnung am Beispiel des Psalm 22* (Munich: Kösel, 1982) 140–43; T. Veijola, "Offenbarung als Begegnung: Von der Möglichkeit einer Theologie des Alten Testaments," *ZTK* 88 (1991) 427–50 (esp. 445–46).

The fact that God's speeches to Job have this *two-fold* purpose becomes clear in Job's two answers to Job. In answer to God's sobering
dethroning of human beings, Job says:

"See, I am of small account; what shall I answer you?" (40:4)

The second purpose, relating to the gospel message that originates in the
very encounter with God and gives meaning to existence, leads Job to the
answer:

"I had heard of you by the hearing of the ear, but now my eye sees
you; therefore I despise myself and repent in dust and ashes."[49]
(42:5–6)

This retraction does not follow in the steps of defeat but is occasioned by
the overwhelming experience of God's presence.[50] In the very moment, in
which Job is given an actually impossible encounter with the living God,
his life is transformed completely. He has learned that he is not at the center of God's activities, and this insight leads him to true wisdom.

---

49. On the problems relating to the translation of 42:5, see I. Willi-Plein, "Hiobs
Widerruf? Eine Untersuchung der Wurzel *nacham* und ihrer erzähltechnischen Funktion
im Hiobbuch," in *Isaac Leo Seeligmann Volume: Essays on the Bible and the Ancient World*
(ed. A. Rofé and Y. Zakovitch; Jerusalem: Rubenstein, 1983) 3:273–89. Willi-Plein suggests
the following translation: "Therefore I have no further request, and I relent [consoled]
concerning earth and dust" ["Deshalb liegt mir nichts mehr daran, und ich bin (tröstlich)
umgestimmt über Erdreich und Staub"]. See also C. Dohmen, "'Mein Gott, mein Gott,
wozu hast du mich verlassen?' (Ps 22,2) Wie die Bibel die Warum-Frage im Leid überwindet," in *Warum, Gott. . . ? Der fragende Mensch vor dem Geheimnis Gottes* (ed. K. J. Lesch
and M. Saller; Kevelaer: Butzon & Bercker, 1993) 12–18 (here 15–16). Dohmen suggests
the following paraphrase: "Therefore I repudiate it, and I repent concern dust and ashes"
["deshalb lehne ich es ab, und es reut mich wegen Staub und Asche"] and explains: "Job,
therefore, recants not of what he just brought as a complaint, but rather, the *experience* of
God's greatness allows him partly to withdraw his questions, which were based on hearsay,
but on the other hand, it vindicates his complaint as trust in the correct authority" ["Ijob
widerruft folglich nicht das, was er gerade erst als Klage vorgebracht hat, sondern die *er-
fahrene* Größe Gottes lässt ihn seine Fragen, dieses vom Hörensagen, quasi zurückziehen,
aber sie rechtfertigt andererseits geradezu seine Klage als Vertrauen in die richtige Instanz"];
E. J. van Wolde, "Job 42,1–6: The Reversal of Job," in *The Book of Job* (ed. W. A. M. Beuken;
BETL 114; Leuven: Peeters, 1994) 223–50, makes a convincing case for retaining a translation that emphasizes Job's inner conversion.
50. The importance of this statement is further emphasized when compared to other
Old Testament texts that reflect on the ability of human beings to encounter God face-to-
face. See C. Dohmen, "'Nicht sieht mich der Mensch und lebt' (Ex 33,20): Aspekte der
Gottesschau im Alten Testament," *Jahrbuch für Biblische Theologie* 13 (1998) 31–51.

CHAPTER 6

The Destination

MANFRED OEMING

1. The Problem: Why Does God Pronounce Someone Innocent Who Had Been Condemned by Everyone? Why Does He Praise Job?

"I am innocent!" (Job 9:21, 33:9). Job has passionately fought for recognition of the fact that his suffering has been a great injustice. The book of Job described the dramatic conflict between the protagonist, his friends, and God through almost 40 chapters. It repeatedly returns to the question of why a perfect God-fearing individual (Job 1:7) fell into such misery. According to all categories of wisdom theology that assume a justifiable causal connection between action and consequences, his fate remains incomprehensible. His story is a scandal that casts grave doubt on God's justice. The three friends attempt to understand how God could remain justified even in the depths of Job's suffering. They pursue different strategies for defending God while consistently maintaining that Job does not speak correctly of God when he accuses him of the indiscriminate use of power, violence, and imposed failure (see 9:22–23). The stirring debate does not lead to agreement; it does not even bring the individual positions closer together. Instead, the arguments are pushed to hardened extremes. At this point, a previously unknown fourth friend enters the debate (Job 32–37) and attempts once more to "explain" why Job is wrong in the way he speaks about God. Finally, God himself enters the stage (chaps. 38–41) and pronounces judgment on Job, albeit gently, with rhetorical questions that all follow the melody of the first:

> Who is this that darkens counsel by words without knowledge? (38:2)

Following this great theophany, in which Job radically recognizes the boundaries of what he can know and accomplish, the protagonist confesses his own guilt (42:1–6):

84

> Therefore I have uttered what I did not understand, things too
> wonderful for me, which I did not know. . . .
> I had heard of you by the hearing of the ear, but now my eye
> sees you;
> therefore I despise myself, and repent in dust and ashes.
> (Job 42:2, 5–6)

Job has been led on a long path toward conversion; he has realized that
he himself was wrong. All of a sudden, however, and in a completely unexpected turn of events, God speaks once more to Job's friends and confronts Eliphaz with this statement:

> My wrath is kindled against you and against your two friends; for
> you have not spoken of me what is right, as my servant Job has.
> (42:7)

This unreservedly positive evaluation of Job as the "servant of God"
stands in glaring contradiction to all that has been said before: Job has
been judged from all sides— the three friends, Elihu, God, and even by
himself—only to have God pronounce him correct in the end? This phe-
nomenon is difficult to comprehend; it is the biggest surprise in the book
of Job[1] and demands that the interpreter bring his entire exegetical virtuosity into play. Even if scholars continually emphasize that these verses are
"key words"[2] for the structure of the entire book, there is great controversy on how they are to be understood. In a second step, we shall look at
the history of scholarship on the book of Job in order to discover possible
aids for understanding this dilemma.

2. An Overview of the Various Solutions Proposed for
This Problem in the History of Scholarship on the Book of Job

The dilemma of the contradiction between sharp criticism (38:2 and
40:8) and high praise of Job by Yahweh (42:7) is noted and discussed in
virtually all commentaries. Stanley Porter and Siegfried Wagner[3] dedicated
entire essays to just this issue in the 1990s. We can distinguish between

---

1. Compare H. Seebass, *Der Gott der ganzen Bibel: Biblische Theologie zur Orientierung im Glauben* (Freiburg: Herder, 1982) 196.
2. See W. Zimmerli, *Grundriß der alttestamentlichen Theologie* (6th ed.; Stuttgart:
Kohlhammer, 1989) 145.
3. S. E. Porter, "The Message of the Book of Job: Job 42:7 as Key to Interpretation,"
EvQ 63 (1991) 291–304; S. Wagner, "Theologischer Versuch über Ijob 42,7–9(10a)," in
Alttestamentlicher Glaube und Biblische Theologie (ed. J. Hausmann and H.-J. Zobel; Stuttgart: Kohlhammer, 1992) 216–24.

several different types of solutions that I would like to summarize in five main groups.

2.1. *The Text-Critical Solution*

One elegant solution when dealing with problems of interpretation is to read the Hebrew text differently. Different suggestions are made for Job 42:7; all are, however, without support in the various manuscripts. The Catholic Old Testament scholar Paul Szczygiel referred to the syntactic structures in Job 3:22, Job 9:22, as well as 2 Sam 23:23. He proposed eliminating a *yod* and reading the following:

> My wrath is kindled against you and against your two friends; for you have not spoken of me *until it was right*, as my servant Job has.

חרה אפי בך ובשני רעיך כי לא דברתם אלי נכונה כעבדי איוב

In this reading, God—just like Elihu in 32:3, 5[4]—is upset at the friends' lack of persistence. He judges them for giving up too quickly without really having won the argument. Job is thus only praised because he did not stop speaking. This "solution," arrived at by presuming an alternate reading of the text, cannot be sustained methodologically; we might consider such an alternate reading if the Masoretic Text were totally corrupt, but this is clearly not the case.

2.2. *The Source-Critical Solution: 42:7 Refers Back to the Beginning of Job's Speeches in Chapters 1 and 2*

The most popular explanation is based on the assumption that verses 42:7–8 belong to a different diachronic layer than the long dialogue passages in chapters 3 to 42:6. Several formal arguments provide legitimacy for the common separation between an (old) folk-tale and a (younger) poetic work: the so-called "narrative framework" is written in prose, the dialogues in poetic language. According to the majority view, the fragmentary "folk-tale" tells of a pious Job, who accepts his suffering and humbly submits himself to God's will, even in the face of most horrible experiences such as the death of his children and serious illness. If we assume with Ernst Würthwein, Gerhard von Rad, Rolf Rendtorff, and my honored teacher Antonius Gunneweg[5] that 42:7 refers directly back to

---

4. "He was angry also at Job's three friends because they had found no answer, though they had declared Job to be in the wrong."

5. E. Würthwein, "Gott und Mensch in Dialog und Gottesreden des Buches Hiob," in *Wort und Existenz: Studien zum Alten Testament* (ed. E. Würthwein; Göttingen: Vandenhoeck & Ruprecht, 1970) 217–95 (here 225); G. von Rad, *Weisheit in Israel* (3rd ed.;

chapter 2, God's praise would be a confirmation, an "honoring" of Job's humble piety described in 1:21 and 2:10:

> The LORD gave, and the LORD has taken away; blessed be the name of the LORD. (1:21)
> If we have received good things of the hand of the Lord, shall we not endure evil things? (2:10)

This attempt at solving the problem is faced, however, with one grave difficulty: it underestimates the literary connections within the text in its final form. The prose frame and the poetic dialogues are connected to a much greater degree than the simple division suggests; this has been especially demonstrated by Jewish students of narrative such as Meir Weiss and Moshe Greenberg.[6] A decisive input gained from the interaction between exegesis and literary/narratological analysis has been the insight that we do not fully understand texts after we have determined their diachronic genesis but only when they have been comprehended in their final form.[7] The source-critical solution also produces—as is often the case—its own problems: according to the narrative frame, the friends say *nothing*. According to Job 2:13, they sat seven days in silent solidarity around a suffering Job. Those who say nothing cannot say something incorrectly, which is precisely what engenders God's anger. We would have to assume that some type of objectionable speech by the friends was lost from the prose framework. The fact that the source-critical hypothesis is based on speculation over lost text and stands in opposition to observations about literary connections between prose and poetry sections is the very reason why it fails to be convincing. Viktor Maag proposed a variation of this hypothesis. He excises the theophany in Job 38–41 as a secondary element and thus attains a close connection between our text and the dialogues: 42:7–9 now appears as the original conclusion of God's speech that arbitrates the dispute between Job and his friends.[8] This answers why God addresses the friends directly, but it leaves the question open as to why they are judged so harshly.

Neukirchen-Vluyn: Neukirchener Verlag, 1985) 269 n. 23, 292; R. Rendtorff, *Das Alte Testament: Eine Einführung* (4th ed.; Neukirchen-Vluyn: Neukirchener Verlag, 1992) 117; A. H. J. Gunneweg, *Biblische Theologie des Alten Testaments* (Stuttgart: Kohlhammer, 1993) 241.

6. M. Weiss, *The Story of Job's Beginning: Job 1–2: A Literary Analysis* (Jerusalem: Magnes, 1983); M. Greenberg, "Job," in *The Literary Guide to the Bible* (2nd ed.; ed. R. Alter and F. Kermode; London: Fontana, 1989) 283–304 (esp. 284–86).

7. M. Oeming and A. R. Pregla, New Literary Criticism, *TRu* 66 (2001) 1–23.

8. V. Maag, *Hiob: Wandlung und Verarbeitung des Problems in Novelle, Dialogdichtung und Spätfassungen* (FRLANT 128; Göttingen: Vandenhoeck & Ruprecht, 1982) 192.

2.3. *The Immediate Context as Solution:*
42:7 Refers to the End of Job's Speech in 42:5–6

If the source-critical approach sought a solution by going all the way back to the chapter two, this solution follows the opposite path and finds answers in the immediate context of God's praise of Job. Job's positive commendation in 42:7 thus only refers to Job's retraction of all his attacks against God in 42:1–6. This solution is rarely followed, but Gustav Hölscher and Georg Fohrer[9] are among those who accept this model. There are several reasons that speak in favor of this option:[10] as part of a lively dialogue, God's praise would thus be a direct reaction to Job's last words (Job's second to last words are quite far away in chapter 31).

Yet, this interpretation still faces the problem that God's wrath against the friends remains without any context. The friends had actually urged Job to retract his statements. They, too, emphasized the greatness and transcendence of God and thus anticipated YHWH's answer to Job. One could make the argument that God, speaking from within the storm, added no new content to what has already been said. If God chastises the friends, he chastises himself.

Another solution is proposed by referring to the theophany in chapter 38. The friends also hear God's speech to Job, but they fail to respond to it; they remained silent in the face of God's words, which occasions God's anger against them. This suggestion, put forward by Stanley Porter,[11] does not seem implausible. I considered it for a long time because it seems to remain close to the wording of the text. As we shall see, however, it is not close enough.

2.4. *Recent Solutions: 42:7 Refers to the Dialogue in Total.*
God's Praise Is a Praise of Rebellion and Protest;
His Anger Is Directed against Theological Conservatism

If it remains implausible to connect God's praise only to the beginning or to the end of the Job's words, then it must refer to the middle

---

9. G. Hölscher, *Das Buch Hiob* (2nd ed.; HAT 17; Tübingen: Mohr, 1952) 4: "When at the end of 42:7 Yahweh is enraged at the friends because they judged falsely about him and places himself on Job's side, this relates clearly to Job's last words of 40:4–5, 42:2–3, 5–6, in which he acknowledged the superiority of the divine power and wisdom [cf. chaps. 38–40] and bows humbly before this recognition" ["Wenn Jahwe am Ende 42:7 gegen die Freunde erzürnt ist, weil sie unrichtig über ihn geurteilt haben, und sich auf Hiobs Seite stellt, so bezieht sich das deutlich auf Hiobs letzte Worte 40,4–5 42,2–3.5–6, in denen er die Überlegenheit der göttlichen Macht und Weisheit (cf. chap. 38–40) anerkennt und sich demütig unter diese Erkenntnis beugt"]; G. Fohrer, *Hiob*, 538–39.

10. See Porter, "The Message of the Book of Job," 298–99.

11. Ibid., 299–300.

and thus to Job's rebellion against God in chaps. 3–31. God's anger, on the other hand, refers to the friends' detailed arguments on why God was justified in his actions. This interpretation dares to assume that God's final words defend Job's borderline blasphemy while judging those who defend God. With his acceptance of Job, God thus does something revolutionary: he justifies those who scream against the injustice in this world and blame it on God's injustice. During the Jounées Bibliques in Leuven in the summer of 1993, and coming from the context of liberation theology, Ulrich Berges entered a passionate plea for the rights of the rebel Job:

> The world was and is in a lamentable situation: Job needs not take anything away from his accusation. . . . Job's theology, deemed heretical, is credited as orthodox by God himself. The theology of the friends, who called on God as the guarantor of a just world order, is revealed to be false. . . . Only now do God's monologues appear as what they truly are: one last test. Job has refused to bow down before God and his friends, this constitutes his greatness. . . . Innocent and unjust suffering is connected directly to God; of this there can be no doubt, following Job. Poverty, sickness, and violent death are not only the results of structural injustice or human failing. Job's leprosy becomes God's leprosy.[12]

The meaning of our verse 42:7 would make the paradoxical statement that God encourages us to protest angrily against him. God stands on the side of those who shout their accusations at God—God against God.

As much as I am attracted to this solution, I see major problems with approaching the dilemma in this manner: It assumes that God's entire speech is intended to be ironic—not a true portrait of God's view of the world, but only a test for Job. This is hard to prove. This overall approach can only work if Job does not condemn himself in 42:5–6. A different translation of Job 42:1–6 becomes necessary. Thus Berges translates the central passage no longer as:

---

12. U. Berges, "Hiob in Lateinamerika: Der leidende Mensch und der aussätzige Gott," in *The Book of Job* (ed. W. A. M. Beuken; BETL 114; Leuven: Peeters, 1994) 297–317 (here 314). ["Die Situation dieser Welt war und ist beklagenswert; von seiner Anklage braucht Hiob keinerlei Abstriche zu machen. . . . Die angeblich häretische Theologie Hiobs wird von Gott selbst also die orthodoxe ausgewiesen. Die Theologie der Freunde, die Gott als Garanten der gerechten Weltlenkung ausgab, wird von Jahwe selbst als falsch entlarvt. . . . Die Gottesreden werden also erst jetzt als das erkenntlich, was sie wirklich sind: eine allerletzte Prüfung. Weder vor den Freunden noch vor Gott hat sich Hiob gebeugt, die ist sein Größe. . . . Unschuldiges und ungerechtes Leiden hat mit Gott selbst zu tun; darüber gibt es seit Hiob keinen Zweifel mehr. Armut, Krankheit und gewaltsamer Tod können weder allein den ungerechten Strukturen noch der menschlichen Schuldhaftigkeit angelastet werden. Der Aussatz Hiobs wird zum Aussatz Gottes."]

Therefore I despise myself, and repent in dust and ashes.

He instead translates:

This is distasteful to me. I refuse to be a part of this and find comfort in dust and ashes.

and explains:

Job does not abandon his position following God's monologues; he does not repent of anything that he had said previously. He remains consistent up to the last moment. . . . Job has consciously decided to take a stance against God and his speeches. His own dialogues with and against his friends had led him to the insight that God was indeed almighty, but unjust. God's monologues only confirmed this position. [13]

This interpretation of Job's answer to God's monologues as a speech that ridicules God as an immoral despot, couched in sarcastic irony, has become quite popular in various versions since Carl Gustav Jung and Ernst Bloch.[14] Even so, I cannot accept this position. As I have argued in detail elsewhere,[15] God's monologues and Job's answers appear to be serious statements.[16] On the one hand we encounter a worthy and weighty presentation of God's superiority that is not bound by anthropocentric categories and, on the other hand, an honest introspection by Job who, *in healthy mortification,* recognizes and accepts his own inferiority. Job does retract! [I cannot discuss in detail the primarily philological problems associated with these verses,[17] but I remain skeptical of whether Job's answer

13. Ibid., 314–15. ["Hiob lenkt am Ende der Gottesreden nicht ein, er bereut überhaupt nichts von dem, was er zuvor behauptet hatte, sondern ist konsequent bis zum letzten Augenblick. . . . Hiob hat sich bewußt gegen Gott und seine Reden entschieden. Wohin ihn die Reden mit oder gegen seine Freunde geführt hatten, zur Einsicht, dass Gott zwar allmächtig, aber ungerecht sei, sieht er nun durch die Gottesreden als bestätigt an."]
14. C. G. Jung, *Antwort an Ijob* (Olten: Walter, 1952) 23, 31; E. Bloch, *Atheismus im Christentum: Zur Religion des Exodus und des Reichs* (stw 144; Frankfurt: Suhrkamp, 1973) 118–34. See also M. H. Pope, *Job* (AB 15; New York: Doubleday, 1973) 348. A recent research survey is provided by J. van Oorschot, "Tendenzen der Hiobforschung," *TRu* 60 (1995) 351–88.
15. M. Oeming, "'Kannst Du der Löwin ihren Raub zu fressen geben?' (Hi 38,39): Das Motiv des 'Herrn der Tiere' und sein Bedeutung für die Theologie der Gottesreden Hi 38–42," in *"Dort ziehen Schiffe dahin. . ."*: Collected Communications to the XIV Congress of the International Organization for the Study of the Old Testament, Paris 1992 (ed. M. Augustin and K. D. Schunck; BEATAJ 28; Frankfurt: Lang, 1996) 147–63.
16. Cf. M. V. Fox, "God's Answer and Job's Response," *Bib* 94 (2013), 1–23.
17. The most detailed attempt to show the "retraction" to be a faulty interpretation of the text by means of philological argument is put forward by I. Willi-Plein, "Hiobs Widerruf?

can only be understood as irony and that all traditional interpretations of the verse are incorrect.] If Job had remained convinced that he is right and God is wrong, even *following* the theophany, then *he* (who is previously known for his radical choice of words) would not make his final statement in such soft tones and vague words, which could easily be (and are!) mistaken for repentance.

I also believe that the negative evaluation of the theology of the friends is problematic, even if most scholars agree on this issue. The friends are highly competent systematic theologians[18] who show great sensitivity

---

Eine Untersuchung der Wurzel *nacham* und *ma'as* und ihrer erzähltechnischen Funktion im Hiobbuch," in *Isaak Leo Seligmann Volume: Essays on the Bible and the Ancient World* (ed. A. Rofé and Y. Zakovitch; Jerusalem: Rubenstein, 1983) 3:273–89. According to Willi-Plein, *nacham* expresses "that a process is initiated from the outside, which leads a subject to rethink a certain subject matter" (283; the verb articulates an "objective fact that leads to a change of attitude"). This basic meaning would then lead to the translations "to be comforted, to seek revenge, to repent, to confirm one's decision," according to the specific context. The verb *ma'as* means "to withdraw one's interest, to express one's lack of interest." Following her philological examination, Will-Plein translates the verse as follows: "Thus I no longer uphold my interest in this subject matter, and I find a (comforting) change of mind in regard to earth and dust."

Despite her very learned arguments, this translation remains tenuous. The meaning of the verbs and all other lexemes are quite open: *ma'as* I means "to hold in contempt" (with an object indicated by *min* or *bĕ*), it is only used absolutely in Ps 89:39, where the text seems to read that God has rejected his anointed. The second entry, *ma'as* II, remains unclear: Job 7:16 = "no longer like?" Job 34:33; 36:5 = "reject"? *nacham* is just as ambiguous: (1) "to feel sorry for/about, to feel remorse"; (2) "to comfort oneself (a Piel reflexive), Ezek 31:16; Ps 77:3; Gen 24:67; Piel: "comfort." The verb thus oscillates between "feel compassion" and "feel remorse." It is also unclear what *'al-'aphar wa'epher* is supposed to mean. Does "over dust and ashes" refer to a locality where Job is sitting, or is it a metaphor for human nature? Because of the uncertain philology of the individual lexemes of this statement, the translations of the whole verse vary to a large degree: "Thus I retract and breathe relief in dust and ashes" (German "Einheitsübersetzung"); "Thus I retract my words and repent in dust and ashes" (German "Elberfelder"); "Thus I reject and I feel remorse because of dust and ashes" (C. Dohmen: "'Mein Gott, mein Gott, wozu hast Du mich verlassen?' (Ps 22,2): Wie die Bibel die Warum-Frage im Leid überwindet," in *Warum Gott . . . ? Der fragende Mensch vor dem Geheimnis Gottes* [ed. K. F. Lesch and M. Saller; Vechtaer Beiträge zur Theologie 2; Kevelaer: Butzon & Berckler, 1993] 12–19 [here 15].) "Thus I retract and repent because I am made of dust and ashes" (M. Witte, *Vom Leiden zur Lehre: Der dritte Redegang (Hiob 21–27) und die Redaktionsgeschichte des Hiobbuches* [BZAW 230; Berlin: de Gruyter, 1994) 176, which refers to the Greek version of Gen 18:27 "I hold myself to be dust and ashes."

I am most convinced by Ellen van Wolde's arguments defending the classical position: "Job 42:1–6: The Reversal of Job," in *The Book of Job* (ed. W. A. M. Beuken; BETL 114; Leuven: Peeters, 1994) 223–50, who moves from the clear to the unclear and argues that the entire scope of the dialogues aims to show how Job is led to accept what he had believed from the beginning, following a long period of doubt.

18. See L. Steiger, "Die Wirklichkeit Gottes in unserer Verkündigung," in *Auf dem Wege zur schriftgemäßer Verkündigung* (ed. M. Honecker and L. Steiger; BEvT 39; Munich: Kaiser, 1965), 143–77 (esp. 157–61; here 161): "The preacher must recognize himself in the friends, . . . They spoke of God when, and as long as, God was silent. This is the very

for pastoral care,[19] and Jürgen Ebach admonishes us: "It is . . . quite odd when theologians villainize theologians for being theologians."[20] Ebach correctly emphasizes the fact that the friends reiterate nothing but what Job had trusted in and believed before he fell ill. (At the same time, Ebach does not exonerate the friends completely; he actually judges them quite harshly in the end. Their faith had become an "ideology" according to which they believe they must defend God, and as a result they force God into their worldview).[21] But is it not hubris when Job claims to be completely without sin? Is it not theologically appropriate to criticize Job and show him how much he, too, is dependent on the grace of God? Are the friends not much closer to Old Testament anthropology in general (see Ps 14:3; 130:3 et al.) than Job, who incessantly defends his self-proclaimed "doctrine" of innocence? These are important questions, but they must be addressed at a different time.

We find a different variation of the modern solution in the work of Christian Weyer, who provided an interpretive rereading of the book of Job in the early 1980s. He connects the divine monologues with the context of the atomic threat during the nuclear arms race. In answer to Job's accusation, God breaks his silence and confesses to Job his desperation over the course of human history, which is soaked in violence and perversion. God says:

> Job, I have seen you,
> as you protested and cried out,
> I have been present at each of your demonstrations
> I carried your banners
> and sung your chants,
> with joy did I listen to your speakers.
> *There* I rediscovered my hope:
> With the priest
> who stands on the side of the poor in the south,

---

situation that theology and proclamation find themselves in every day. Woe be to the theologian and preacher who first identifies himself with Job and criticizes the friends for their shortcomings, only because he cannot stand their situation, which is also his own!"

19. See V. Weymann, "Hiob," in *Geschichte der Seelsorge in Einzelportraits* (ed. C. Möhler; Göttingen: Vandenhoeck & Ruprecht, 1994) 1:35–53; T. Mickel, *Seelsorgerliche Aspekte im Hiobbuch* (Leipzig: Evangelische Verlagsanstalt, 1990).

20. J. Ebach, "Gott und die Normativität des Faktischen: Plädoyer für die Freunde Hiobs," in *Hiobs Post: Gesammelte Aufsätze zu Hiobbuch, zu Themen biblischer Theologie und zur Methodik der Exegese* (ed. J. Ebach; Neukirchen-Vluyn: Neukirchener Verlag, 1995) 55–66 (here 55). ["Es mutet . . . seltsam an, wenn Theologen Theologen als Theologen diffamiern."]

21. Ibid., 62–63.

with the teacher,
who refuses his thoughts to be imprisoned,
with the worker,
who demands just pay for his work,
with the young and the old,
who protest against A-, B-, and C-weapons,
with all those,
who condemn nuclear power and the destruction of the
    environment.
Job, *you* are my hope and my hands,
you can spare this world,
in accordance to my plan.
That is why I ask you, Job:
Stand up and do not allow words to tear you apart,
spoken by friends who have not understood.
. . .
If you and those like you give up,
there is no more hope for me.[22]

---

22. C. Weyer, *Hiobs-botschaft* (Stuttgart: Radius, 1993) 23–24.

["Hiob, ich habe euch gesehen,
wie ihr protestiert und aufgeschrieen habt,
jede eurer Demonstrationen begleite ich,
ich habe eure Transparente mitgetragen
und eure Parolen mitgesungen,
mit Freunden hörte ich euren Rednern zu.
Dort habe ich meine Hoffnung wiedergefunden:
Bei dem Priester,
der im Süden die Partei der Armen ergreift,
bei dem Lehrer,
der sein Gehirn nicht einkerkern lassen will,
bei dem Arbeiter,
der gerechten Lohn für seine Arbeit fordert,
bei den Jungen und Alten,
die gegen A-, B-, und C-Waffen demonstrieren,
bei all denen,
die Atomkraft und Umweltzerstörung verdammen.
Hiob, *ihr* seid meine Hoffnung,
ihr seid meine Arme und meine Hände,
ihr könnt die Welt bewahren,
so wie es meinem Plan entspricht.
Deshalb bitte ich dich nun, Hiob:
Stehe auf und lass dich nicht zerreden
von deinen Freunden, die nicht verstanden haben.
. . .
Wenn du und deinesgleichen resignieren,
gibt es keine Hoffnung mehr für mich."]

Rebellion is given divine approval in 42:7. But does this interpretation not mirror the spirit of the time in which it was written instead of the spirit of the text it aims to understand? Do we not have to distinguish between original intent and later use of the text? Job as a protester with a megaphone leading a demonstration in central Heidelberg—is this what 42:7 really means? I do not think so. The text describes a diseased and decaying man who is engaged in an intense debate with his friends. The text does not seem to give wholesale approval of rebellion against injustice in this world—be it *against* God (thus Berges) or *with* God (thus Weyer). The criticism of Job's "words without understanding" and Job's "turning in dust and ashes" are stated too clearly.

2.5. *A Compromise: 42:7 Refers Only to Individual Aspects of the Dialogues*

If we cannot praise Job's speeches *in toto*, then it must be possible to connect the divine evaluation to individual aspects articulated by the speeches or individual aspects of the dialogue itself. This assumption has also led to various hypotheses.

Josef Schreiner believes that Job is correct when he emphasizes the notion that the assumption of a causal connection between action and consequence was illusory; God is always free in his actions. Yet Job misunderstands God's freedom as arbitrary power. Now he discovers that God is also free to not punish him but to grant him everything once again in double measure.[23] I find this interpretation to be unsatisfying because it diminishes the problem inherent in the clear praise given to Job.

Job's strength has also been seen in his insistence on trusting his own experience more than what *is said* in general. Job did not fall back onto common assumptions but held fast to his own insight into reality. We could assume with Horst Seebass that the verse explains how Job wrestles with God against an image of God and never gives up.[24] Or we state that Job was indeed correct when proclaiming that his suffering was not directly caused by his own actions.

On the other hand, the decisive mistake made by Job's friends is seen in their exaggeration of the causal connection between action and consequence.

Various exegetes have echoed similar thoughts: Pope, *Job*, 350: "God values the integrity of the impatient protester."

23. J. Schreiner, *Theologie des Alten Testaments* (NEB Ergänzung 1; Würzburg, Echter, 1995) 181.

24. H. Seebass, *Der Gott der ganzen Bibel*, 196.

They are quite serious in their defense of God's actions and say much that is valuable; but in all this they speak about God as if there were no secret within God, as if human beings could fully understand him. In the face of God they know not of lament or of question and are thus mistaken about the truth of God and the truth of human existence.[25]

The wise men teach us that all those who act badly will end badly. Job's friends dared to turn this statement around and defend it with growing urgency: because Job ended badly, he must have acted badly.[26] Axel Graupner has pointed this out and interprets Job 42:7 as follows: "In the end, the book of Job explicitly criticizes a kind of piety that believes it must protect itself with pious phrases from the abyss that is God himself."[27] Any inference from a fate back to its possible cause leads astray when it overlooks that the suggested causal connection can never be a closed system. Bernd Janowski has shown well that, even though God has an important function in conceptualizing retribution, this function can never be reduced to an automatic mechanism.[28] God himself is the third element, in addition to the action and the acting subject; God also retains the freedom to disrupt the connection between the other two or to enforce it.

Even though these interpretations all have their strengths, we are still left with the problem that Porter has articulated clearly:[29] *every* reduction of a specific aspect that may have been the cause of God's praise or criticism implies certain external assumptions. The text itself remains open.

---

25. A. Jepsen, *Das Buch Hiob und seine Deutung* (AzTh I/14; Stuttgart: Calwer, 1963) 24. ["Sie meinen es gewiß sehr ernst mit ihrer Rechtfertigung Gottes und sagen manches gute Wort; aber in alledem reden sie über Gott, als gäbe es bei Gott keine Geheimnisse, als könne der Mensch Gottes Handeln durchschauen. Sie haben im Grunde vor Gott weder Klage noch Frage und verkennen damit die Wirklichkeit Gottes ebenso wie die Wirklichkeit des menschlichen Lebens."]

26. This becomes most clear in Eliphaz's last speech, in which he insinuates that Job must have committed heinous crimes (Job 22:5–9).

27. Unpublished lecture manuscript. ["Das Hiobbuch enthält zum Schluß eine explizite Kritik an einer Frömmigkeit, die meint, sich mit Lehrsätzen gegen den Abgrund schützen zu können, der Gott selber ist. "]

28. B. Janowski, "Die Tat kehrt zum Täter zurück, Offene Fragen im Umkreis des 'Tun-Ergehen-Zusammenhangs,'" *ZTK* 91 (1994) 247–71. Cf. M. Oeming, "Behinderung als Strafe? Zum biblisch fundierten seelsorglichen Umgang mit dem Tun-Ergehen-Zusammenhang," in *Behinderung–Profile inklusiver Theologie, Diakonie und Kirche* (ed. J. Eurich and A. Lob-Hüdepohl; Behinderung–Theologie–Kirche 7; Stuttgart: Kohlhammer 2014), 98–126.

29. "It is a misguided effort to say which specific words of Job are correct. The text is not more specific regarding which exact words are referred to by God" (ibid., 303).

If we summarize our survey of the various interpretations suggested in the recent history of scholarship, then we end with a degree of despair: None of the suggested explanations are fully satisfactory. The solution suggested last may be the most convincing, but even it falls short. Will this verse remain a *crux interpretum*, or can a new look at the text lead us to a solution?

3. My Suggestion: A New Translation of 42:7: Using the Direction of Speech as a Criterion of Theology

It is one of the rare moments of joy in the life of an exegete when he notices something in a text that he and others had not noticed before. This is what happened to me in my reading of the conclusion to the book of Job. There came a point when I noticed that the usual translation of 42:7–8 could not be correct. Most often, the decisive phrase is translated:

> . . . for you have not spoken *of me* what is right, as my servant Job has.[30]

This translation has its equivalent in various English versions (NKJV, NAS, NIV) as well as in other languages. Examples are: "vous n'avez par parlé *de moi avec droiture* comme l'a fait mon servituer Job" (Nouvelle Edition Genève 1979) or "denn ihr habt nicht recht *von mir* geredet wie mein Knecht Hiob" (Luther 1984, Buber 1962, Einheitsübersetzung 1980, Schlechter 1951). All translations emphasize that Job spoke correctly *about* God, whereas his friends did not.

Nonetheless, let us look closely at the text. The phrase דברתם אל is ambiguous, to say the least. The preposition אל occurs 5,464 times in the Old Testament;[31] BDB defines its meaning as "denoting motion to or direction toward (whether physical or mental).[32] It seems to me that the basic meaning of the preposition is 'in relation to', which is then specified by the immediate context. A wide range of possible meanings thus emerge from the phrase: "You have not spoken correctly in relation to me." The usual translation "spoken about me" is no doubt possible. But is it plausible?

30. Thus the translation in NRSV.
31. According to A. Evan-Shoshan, *A New Concordance of the Bible* (Jerusalem: Kiryat Sepher, 1989) 67.
32. BDB, 39. Cf. Gen 20:2: "Abraham said of his wife Sarah, 'She is my sister.'"; Jer 40:16: "Do not do such a thing, for you are telling a lie about Ishmael."

In the book of Job, the preposition occurs 76 times.[33] Of these 76 instances, most occur in connection with verbs of speech.

In connection with *dibber*, the preposition occurs 9 times;[34] in each instance the preposition means 'to speak to'. This is also clear in the immediate context of our phrase in 42:7a:

> After the LORD had spoken these words *to* Job, the LORD said *to* Eliphaz the Temanite

In connection with the verb *'amar*, the preposition occurs 11 times.[35] These observations lead me to conclude that a verb of speech in connection with אל not only means 'to speak to' in 42:7a (twice!) but also in 42:7b.[36] As a result, however, our problem appears in an entirely new light:

> My wrath is kindled against you and against your two friends; for you have not correctly[37] spoken *to me*, as my servant Job has.

---

33. Of these, 49 are without a suffix. The suffixes are distributed as follows: 6× 1st sg., 5× 2nd m.sg., 13× 3rd m.sg, 1× 3rd f.sg, 3× 3rd m.pl. The 1st and 2nd person plural do not occur.

34. Because this observation is of great importance for my argument, I will briefly list the passages: 2:13: The three friends sat with him on the ground for seven days and seven nights; no one spoke a word to him. 4:2: You (Job) may not like it, when we try to speak to you. 4:12: A word came to me in secret, my ear received a whisper from it. 13:3: I will speak to the Almighty; to argue with God is my desire. 40:27: Does it (Behemoth) beg mercy from you? Does it speak gentle words to you? 42:7a, 7b, 8, 9: After the LORD had spoken these words to Job, the LORD said to Eliphaz the Temanite: "My wrath is kindled against you and against your two friends, for you have not spoken to/of me what is right, as my servant Job has. Now therefore take seven bulls and seven rams, and go to my servant Job, and offer up for yourselves a burnt offering. And my servant Job shall pray for you, for I will accept his prayer not to deal with you according to your folly; for you have not spoken of me what is right, as my servant Job has done." So Eliphaz the Temanite and Bildad the Shuhite and Zophar the Naamathite went and did what the LORD had told them; and the LORD accepted Job's prayer.

35. 1:7: Yahweh spoke to the *satan*. 1:8: Yahweh spoke to the *satan*. 1:12: Yahweh spoke to the *satan*. 2:2: Yahweh spoke to the *satan*. 2:3: Yahweh spoke to the *satan*. 2:6: Yahweh spoke to the *satan*. 2:10: He (Job) spoke to her. 9:12: Who will say to God: What are you doing? 10:2: I say to God. 34:31: If someone says to God. Alongside these passages, we also find the phrase *'amar lĕ* (28:28, 34:18), also with the meaning 'to speak to'.

36. The fact that אל can also mean 'speak against' (see 33:13 in connection with *rib*) might be part of this passage as well, implying that Job spoke to God against God. But this interpretation cannot be based solely on philological arguments.

37. The Niphal participle *neḥonah* can be understood as an adverbial accusative; see (*GKC* §100), who list types of adverbial phrases and state: "Adjectives, especially in their feminine form (as the equivalent of the indogermanic neutrum), such as ראשנה primum/earlier; רבה multum/many, enough." See also R. Meyer, *Hebräische Grammatik III: Satzlehre* (Berlin: de Gruyter, 1972) §105c. If we understand אל as the indication of the direction of speech, then such an interpretation of the accusative becomes necessary.

The plausibility of this translation is increased by the old versions. The Septuagint reads: ἥμαρτες σὺ καὶ οἱ δύο φίλοι σου οὐ γὰρ ἐλαλήσατε ἐνώπιόν μου
ἀληθὲς οὐδέν. Literally, this translates as: "You have sinned, you and your
two friends, for you have not spoken truthfully *in my presence.*" The phrase
ἐνώπιόν μου places the emphasis on the fact that the friends spoke without
being conscious of the fact that they were in the presence of God.[38] True
theology only occurs within this horizon. The Vulgate translates, perhaps
not merely as a translation dependent on the Septuagint: *iratus est furor
meus in te et in duos amicos tuos quoniam non estis locuti coram me rectum
sicut servus meus Iob.* According to the Vulgate, the decisive aspect of the
friends' speech is the personal relation expressed in *coram.*

Thus I come to the conclusion, based on an analysis of the Masoretic
Text and supported by the ancient versions, that God does not praise a
specific statement made by Job (neither the patient sufferer of the beginning, the passionate rebel of the middle section, nor the individual
who rebukes himself in the end). God does not justify a specific *teaching*
about himself but rather the *direction of Job's speech,* his internal stance, his
knowledge of the place to which and from which his thoughts proceed.
God praises Job's speech as a speech *to God.* In contrast, the friends are
not scolded for *what* they have said, but for their attitude toward God. It
is their distant stance toward God that incurs God's wrath: Job's friends
are studious and earnest theologians. They use their full cognitive compe-
tence and produce an impressive system of thought. Yet their mistake lies
in the foundation of their theology: "You have not spoken well *to me,* not
toward me, not *in personal relation to me.* Instead, you only spoke *of me.*
In this, all theology is perverted, becomes sinful, and incurs God's wrath."
Job may speak against God and perhaps even make mistakes, but he speaks
to God and thus receives God's praise. We can describe the paradigmatic
form of Job's speech with a phrase coined by Martin Luther: "contra deum
in deum," to speak against God to God.[39] The friends' error lies in their

---

38. And, truth be told, nowhere in the book do the friends speak to God (unless I
have missed something), even though Job repeatedly admonishes them to do so (see 5:8;
8:5–6; 22:23–25)! Throughout the dialogue, Job, on the contrary, speaks passionately to
God directly.

39. Taken from Luther's commentary on Jonah from 1526 (*WA* 19, 223): "Es kan
natur nicht anders thun noch sich schicken, den wie sie fulet. Nu sie aber Gottes zorn und
straffe fulet, helt si nicht anders von Gott denn als von eym tyrannen, kan sich nicht uber
solchen zorn schwingen odder uber soch fulen springen und durch hyn widder Gott zu Gott
dringen und ruffen." (Nature neither can do differently nor can behave differently than how
it feels. If it feels God's wrath and punishment, it only views God as a tyrant; it cannot vault
themselves above such wrath or jump above such feelings and plead and call through them
against God to God.)

objectified speech; they never speak to God! Instead of prayerfully speaking *to* God and wrestling *with* God, they practice theology as speech about God. Instead of praying *for* Job or *with* Job, they theorize *about* God. In this manner, they completely miss God, even if they do make theologically correct statements.[40]

4. Critical Comments on the Modern Practice of Theology Based on the Text

If we take God's final statement seriously, then theology may not turn into a construct of objectified rational thought. Speaking *to* God does not end in "verbal virtuosity about God" or as an intellectual high-wire act. It is true that theology as scholarship must also speak objectively about God, and it must rely on the tools and methods of intellectual rigor to accomplish this task—but this is not its strength, its pride, or its very nature; instead, this is its weakness, its tragedy, its very failing. It *must* take this circuitous route based on its tragic entanglement, but it must lead back to its true purpose: speaking *to* God in faith. Only if theology, proceeding from speech to God as its source, follows and practices intellectual and scholarly rigor in order to return to this source will it find its true nature. This connection to a living conversation partner makes theology different from other disciplines, such as comparative religious studies or the history of religion.

This source and this destination shines into all subdisciplines of theology: theologians only practice a correct ethos of exegesis in connection to the living God,[41] a connection that is not reduced to objectified speech about the text, but a life with the text.[42] Rudolph Bultmann, one of my theological teachers, made the classic statement:

---

40. Later, I found other scholars holding the same opinion, such as P. van Hecke, "From Conversation about God to Conversation with God: The Case of Job," in *Theology and Conversation: Towards a Relational Theology* (ed. J. Haers and P. de Mey; Leuven: Peeters 2003), 115–24, esp. 118–20 (he argues on the basis of the old translations, esp. the Targum to Job); D. B. Burrell, *Deconstructing Theodicy: Why Job Has Nothing to Say to the Puzzled Suffering* (Grand Rapids: Brazos 2008), 124; C. L. Seow, *Job 1–21* (Illuminations; Grand Rapids; Eerdmans 2013), 92, 500.

41. As a young student, I shook my head when reading how St. Augustine would interject prayers into his exegetical writings. Is this not bad scholarship? Based on my understanding of the book of Job today I would say: No! This is the very foundation that allows true interaction with the text and the reality contained in it.

42. See also C. Sini, "Die Ethik der Auslegung," in *Beiträge zur Hermeneutik aus Italien* (ed. F. Bianco; Alber-Reihe Philosophie; Freiburg: Alber, 1993) 141–57, who makes "living in the text" the foundation of all appropriate hermeneutic.

Adam's sin did not consist of transgressing God's command and
eating the fruit, but in entertaining the question: "Might God
really have said. . . ?" This *disputare de deo* takes a stance outside
of God and makes God's claim on human beings a matter of dispute. . . . Any *talking about* assumes a stance outside of what is
talked about. Yet a stance outside of God cannot exist and we thus
cannot speak of God in general statements or universal truths that
claim to be true without considering the specific existential situation of the speaker.[43]

Once we accept that we must "do" theological scholarship *coram deo*, as
an inescapable fact, our entire paradigm shifts. We encounter a call to the
very subject matter that is a personal other. This leads us to continual reflection and self-criticism: do I know in whose presence I am standing? Do
I know to whom I am *responsible* with my historical reconstructions, my
didactic, homiletic, and poimenic theories, my dogmatic and philosophical systems? Theology is the answer. If we look at modern neo-liberal or
postmodern theology, the question may be raised whether this claim is
valid. Following Gerhard Ebeling, I would like to make a case for Job 42:7
and propose: "Prayer is the hermeneutical key to understanding God. We
understand the being and the attributes of God from a position of prayer."
"If it is true that we can only decide in prayer who God is and understand
our relationship to him, then it follows that the nature of God cannot be
the object of neutral analysis and objectified conclusion."[44] "Thus we may
refer to prayer as the syntax of faith."[45] Non-relational speech, even when
it makes correct statements in weighty and aesthetically pleasing language,
is the *proton pseudos*. Like an inverted Midas curse, it transforms all valu-

---

43. R. Bultmann, "Welchen Sinn hat es, von Gott zu reden?" *Glauben und Verstehen*
(Tübingen 1993) 1:26–37, 26–28. ["dass Adam's Sünde nicht eigentlich die tat, mit der er,
von der verbotenen Frucht essend, das Gebot übertrat, sondern dies, dass er sich einließ auf
die Frage: Sollte Gott gesagt haben? das *'disputare de deo'*, das sich außerhalb Gottes stellen
und den Anspruch Gottes auf den Menschen zum disputablen Problem machen. . . . Denn
jedes *'Reden über'* setzt einen Standpunkt außerhalb dessen, worüber geredet wird, voraus.
Einen Standpunkt außerhalb Gottes aber kann es nicht geben, und von Gott lässt sich deshalb auch nicht in allgemeinen Sätzen, allgemeinen Wahrheiten reden, die wahr sind ohne
Beziehung auf die konkrete existentielle Situation des Redenden."]
44. G. Ebeling, *Dogmatik des christlichen Glaubens 1* (4th ed.; Tübingen: Mohr, 2012),
204. ["Das Phänomen des Gebets wird somit zum hermeneutischen Schlüssel der Got-
teslehre. Von da aus öffnet sich das Verständnis für das Gott zugesprochene Sein und für die
Gott zugesprochenen Attribute." "Wenn es zutrifft, dass am Gebet herauskommt, was es um
das Gottesverhältnis ist, dann ergibt sich daraus, dass Gott wesenhaft nicht zum Gegenstand
neutraler Einstellung werden kann, dass er nicht objektivierbar ist."]
45. See Ebeling, *Dogmatik,* 210. ["Deshalb könnte man das Gebet die Syntax des
Glaubens nennen."]

able theological gold into worthless stuff, all speech about God into "the kind of God-babble that is deplored in the heavens."[46] We all must reflect repeatedly[47] on whether our theology has lost its source and its destination and mutated into "God-babble," for which we too may face God's wrath—because we did not speak *to him* like his servant Job.

Epilogue

At the end of his journey, Job returns to a place that is strangely similar to his departure point, the point from which his entire drama started. He stands in front of us as the exemplary pious individual who performs sacrifices for others. Just as he was concerned for his children, he now concerns himself with his friends (1:5 // 42:8). Job's fate is restored (42:10–17)—his possessions and his blessings, his children and his social standing are not merely returned; they are doubled. The end result seems like the beginning. And yet everything is different. No one walks away from an encounter with illness and death and remains unchanged. Once the very foundations of our existence have been shaken, we no longer take things for granted; life appears in a new light. We only learn true human greatness and maturity through the encounter with the dark sides of human existence. The fact that the burden of Job's journey did not break him is a sign of God's guidance and merciful care.

46. H. Timm, *Sage und Schreibe: Inszenierungen religiöser Lesekultur* (Innen & Außen 2; Kampen: Kok Pharos, 1995) 61 ["das im Himmel unterträgliche Gottesgeschwätz"].

47. On theological reflection, see H. Timm, *Wahr-Zeichen: Angebote zur Erneuerung religiöser Symbolkultur* (Stuttgart 1993) 155–59.

Index of Authors

Index of Scripture

New Testament

Lightning Source UK Ltd.
Milton Keynes UK
UKHW011254281021
392745UK00009B/184